Standing at the Door

The journey of an Indian girl
in the Western world

by
Pushpa Vaghela

Ecademy Press
6 Woodland Rise, Penryn, Cornwall TR10 8QD, UK
info@ecademy-press.com • www.ecademy-press.com

© 2007 Pushpa Vaghela. All rights reserved.

ISBN: 978-1-905823-23-9
ISBN: 1-905823-23-1

First published 10/09/2007 by Ecademy Press

Printed and Bound by:
Lightning Source in the UK and USA

Printed on acid-free paper from managed forests. This book is printed on demand, so no copies will be remaindered or pulped.

The right of Pushpa Vaghela to be identified as the author of this work has been asserted in accordance with Sections 77 and 78 of the Copyright Designs and Patents Act 1988.

A CIP catalogue record for this book is available from the British Library.

All rights reserved. No part of this publication may be reproduced in any material form (including photocopying or storing in any medium by electronic means and whether or not transiently or incidentally to some other use of this publication) without the written permission of the copyright holder except in accordance with the provisions of the Copyright, Design and Patents Act 1988. Applications for the copyright holder's written permission to reproduce any part of this publication should be addressed to the publishers.

Acknowledgements

I wish to acknowledge my soul mother, the late Patricia Stacy. Her words of encouragement and her faith in me never once faltered, she was and still is my guardian angel.

My children for walking beside me, trusting and believing even when I doubted myself. My children are my left and my right hand, they are my tower of pride and if it were not for them I would not have had the will to carry on.

Foreword

It is a great privilege to write the foreword for this book written by an amazing lady. This breathtaking story by Pushpa Vaghela takes you on an intimate, inspirational and heartfelt journey through events in her life. Her story not only gives you a true essence of the peaks and falls of life but also the character that you can build from any type of past trauma and still come out the other side victorious and fulfilled.

I have had the great fortune of watching Pushpa's incredible journey over the last few years and was astonished and inspired by the swift turnaround she made in her life. She not only liberates herself but empowers everyone around her to live their life to a standard beyond imagination. By indulging in this extraordinary lady's story, you begin to take a look at your own life from a different perspective as you begin to realise what is right now.

In this book, Pushpa brings what seems impossible to reality for all of us. Demonstrating that no matter how traumatic lifes events have been in the past, tomorrow can always be a day of transformation.

Personally for me, Pushpa has been a true friend, and a great role model in many ways. Of Pushpa's many qualities, some of the things I truly admire are her transparency, integrity, contribution, and her love for humanity. Pushpa has raised the bar in all areas of her life by turning adverse experiences in her life into gifts. She is not only a phenomenal coach, mum, friend and inspirational leader in her community, she also possesses a soul that elegantly encapsulates your heart by her words and mere presence.

The message from this book will become something very infectious and will create massive change in all areas of our society. I can guarantee that this book will transform, empower and educate not only those who read it, but all those that its readers go on to touch.

Pa Joof,
Coach, Mentor, Millionaire and Anthony Robbins Trainer

Dedication

My Mum and Dad for giving me the chance to live a challenging yet wonderful life and for passing on the tiniest amount of their wisdom to me, thank you so much for allowing me to be your special daughter.

My darling husband Chandra as he gave me the opportunity to be loved and to love unconditionally. My first and everlasting love, I did it darling, I did it!

Introduction

I have seen myself doing many things but writing a book never once crossed my mind until about a year ago. I thought of my journey and realised that I am not the only Asian woman, or any other person in fact, that has been faced with challenges. On many occasions having thought that there is nobody at all in this world that can help him or her. But that is so not true, first of all you need to acknowledge that you do need help, that there is nothing wrong in seeking it and actually take the step to find it, be it via friends, professional groups or any other source.

Life is too short to be discarded. Begging for an end to it when there are people out there who desperately want to live, cannot be justified. This book is a journey as such; it will take you through the times when a child thought that her world was perfect and had her whole future planned out in front of her. The decisions, shifts and sacrifices she felt she had to make in order to live the life she was expected to live. Confused many times, she still carried on and on, only giving in to the solace of her daunting room to cry tears from a bottomless well.

Read her journey, about her losses of her dearest loved ones and her continuous fight knowing that there was a special path that her Creator had made for her, yet fearing to take a step towards it as many of us do. She finally took the hint that was thrown at her many times and made the move. The move meant breaking away from everyone and everything that she had known all her life, taking too the lives most dear to her into the unknown.

Contents

1. The First Door Closes 1
2. Unlocking The Door 15
3. Stepping Through The Door 31
4. The Door I Chose To Open 45
5. The Door Is Open 53
6. The Heaviest Door 65
7. Demons At The Door 77
8. The Door Slams Shut 89
9. Going Inside 103
10. Opportunity Knocks 117
11. The Door To A New Life 127
12. Many Doors 131
13. The Door Into The Future 139

ONE

The First Door Closes

All I had ever wanted was a fun childhood. For me this meant friends, exciting experiences at school, at home, and the best loving respectable and supportive relationship with my family and the special unique bond with my parents.

I used to see what my friends had during my visits to their homes. I remember thinking 'OK, so I don't have the right school kit or better clothes, but I love what I have because they were bought by my mum.' Even so, some day soon I saw myself having as much as my friends. Some day soon. This thought kept me going.

I used to go to my friends' houses to play after school in the summer. They had smaller families than mine. I had nine brothers and two sisters. They were – from the eldest – two brothers, two sisters, five brothers, me and then two more brothers. Mo, Wills, Dev, Shiv, Ash, Govind, Manish, Pradip and Chandan are my brothers. Ursula and Lalita are my sisters. The age difference between most of us is 1 to 2 years but the difference between my eldest brother and me is sixteen years. We also had a stepsister from my father's first marriage.

I had amazing brothers with each one of them having totally differing personalities. Let me introduce you, starting from with Mo, the eldest, who lived life to the full and was very clever. Wills was a lot like my father and quite serious yet very active. These two came to England the year that I was born so that they could set the foundation for the rest of us when we came. Following them my father came with the next two brothers in line and then my mother and the rest of us followed.

Ursula was clever, but I did not really have the opportunity to spend a lot of time with her as she was married by the time I was six years old. I thought she was excellent though because she used to buy me amazing clothes when she came to visit! My favourite dress was a purple one with a gold belt and a black and red poncho, which I wore for forever. I suppose she made it easier for my mum so that my mum did not have go out especially to buy girls clothes for me.

Lalita was fun, loving, and yet anxious. Dev was very serious and loved Elvis, Shiv was fun and did a lot funny silly things. Ash was the experimental cook and probably the most caring, he used to prepare my tea for me in the morning before I used to leave for work and obviously helped a lot around the kitchen. In fact, all my brothers are excellent whether it be in household chores or cooking a meal. Govind was the clever one and the only one to have got to university. Manish loved his food, but was a tower for my father and us when we needed him. Then it's me 10th in line and this is my story. Pradip was very adventurous and would get us worried at times with his tactics, he was the first one to smoke in addition to my father who smoked a pipe and my two eldest brothers. Finally the baby, Chandan, who never learnt to tie his shoe laces till he was well in his teens and an amazing character.

I can't even begin to imagine what my mum must have gone through whilst carrying us all, having only a few months break in between. There was another brother that had died at birth hence my mother had thirteen pregnancies by the time she was 36 years of age.

Even though we did not have the luxuries that my friends or others had and our lives were not perfect in many ways, we did have a lot of love between us all. The love I had for my mother was so special to me, I find it hard to describe in words, it was a feeling that, each time I looked at her, made my face light up and my eyes sparkle.

I wanted to spend every moment of my day with Mum. I did try to spend as much time as possible with her, from the moment I got up and she combed my long hair to sneaking into her bed at night and sleeping curled up at her feet. When I was not with her physically, in mind and spirit my thoughts were of her. During school I could not wait to rush home to her. She was my God, my creator, my world, my everything.

Although we were happy in a lot of ways, my mother worked very hard to provide for us all. It was the smiles on her face all of the time that made us happy. But I knew that Mum used to be constantly worried about money, about us and more so about my fathers drinking habits.

I don't know much about what happened before my earliest memory at the age of about seven, other than what I use to overhear from conversations between my parents, the elder brothers and sisters and the relations that used to come and visit us and tell us about the times back then and how things were.

I learned that my father had been a very talented man, making things from leather in Africa, where he had generated a lot of business. We were all born in Nairobi (in Kenya), apart from my youngest brother who was born in England. My parents originated from India, Gujarat; my mother from a village called Ghara and my father from a village called Umbhel. They had a lot of land there, which my father, being the eldest son of three, inherited. He had passed on the responsibility for looking after this land to his youngest brother when he left India to pursue his dream.

His youngest brother – my uncle – regarded my father as a father figure and kept all the title deeds in my father's name to his dying day. The 12 of us will inherit this land, eventually.

I believe that I have a lot of my father's passion for success. I know that I have the power within me to achieve my dreams. But this book is not about that time; it is about my life's journey so far and about me.

I want to tell you about that journey and show you that whatever you set your heart on is achievable. I only learnt this a year ago and, in the process, found that I had been doing it all along, but for the wrong reasons. Although I had my dreams, I always put other people and their feelings and wants first.

Let's start at the beginning. My earliest memory is from the age of seven, just before my sister's wedding.

I remember going to school and wanting to rush home because my mum was going to take me shopping for an outfit for the wedding. The whole day was spent thinking about it! I was so excited as it was not very often I got new clothes, they were usually handed down from my older sisters, or clothes that were given to the family by other people. I specifically remember a couple that owned a clothes shop that would regularly come and give Mum clothes.

As soon as the bell went I said goodbye to my friends and I ran home as fast as my legs would carry me.

Huffing and puffing I got home to find my mother waiting. We left immediately and I held Mum's hand all the way, as usual. When we reached the tailors house I got measured for a top and bottoms. This was the first time I had ever had clothes made especially for me, it made me feel extra special and I loved it.

I clearly remember the woman telling my mother that she would give her the outfit at a really good deal, awesome! I had a big grin on my face all the way home.

On the day before the wedding Mum also let me wear a pair of 22 carat real gold earrings, I felt rich like a princess and I wore them to school. Whilst playing in the playground during break I lost one of them. When I realised I started crying because I knew how much my mum had struggled to pay for these and I could not even begin to imagine the hurt this would cause her. I dreaded seeing the look of horror on her face if she found out. My friends Susan and Gillian helped me look, but we did not find it.

So I started to cry more and felt very sick, the teacher on duty saw us and came around, we told her what had happened and she started to help us look for it. She found it near the area where we were playing;

I was so relieved and happy. I just wanted to go home, show my mum I still had them on, wear them for the wedding and give them back to my mum as soon as possible for safe keeping. They were my special earrings with green and pink gemstones, which I still have today and will keep forever. I plan to hand them down to my children as my heirloom to them.

Before the wedding I remember my mother having a conversation about being worried how we were going to pay for the wedding and the dowry that the boy's family were asking for. I was very young, so it was really hard for me to understand why she was so worried, but made me sad to see her unhappy.

I knew my mum wanted my sister to have the best, but also knew what a long trek, financially, it was going to be. It is an Asian tradition for the boy's family to ask for a dowry of any value they like. In India wives are still tormented, tortured or burned alive if their families do not give what is asked for. The girls family will go to any lengths to raise the dowry, as they think it as bad for a girl to be at home and single all her life. That is one of the reasons why, when females are born, they are frowned upon. Parents of girls usually start saving up for their wedding day as soon as they are born.

I remember going shopping with Mum and buying all the things we needed on credit as usual, promising the shopkeepers that she will pay them a bit on a weekly basis, that credit tab never ended.

Every week I would go shopping for our food with Mum and helping her to bring it home. She would carry the shopping box on her shoulder and it was a very hilly walk back home. I remember thinking that when I got older and it was my time to get married, I won't, because I had already made my mind up to stay with Mum forever. I was never ever going to leave her.

The thought that I would make sure that she would never have to ask for credit again were always running through my head. I would have a car so that she would not have to carry the shopping in a box on her shoulder all the way home, I would sometimes look at her and it she looked as if she was carrying the weight of the world. Gosh, she was one strong lady.

I can't remember the exact age I started going to work with my mother after school, but it was very soon after the wedding. It started with her evening job in the town centre. We would catch the bus and go into town to clean offices. I remember cleaning out the ashtrays and emptying the dustbins for her. She used to have a white and lilac overall.

On Fridays we used to go shopping for things on offer in the town. I remember carrying home bags of sugar, sometimes as many as twelve 1kg packets. I also remember her lilac summer coat, which I loved because it had deep pockets. The reason for this was that when my mum used to hold my hand, the pockets were so deep that she used to put both our hands in her pocket and that is how we used to go everywhere. I loved it feeling her warm hand around mine, and running along side of her, she was a fast walker. I think that is why my favorite colour is purple and I walk really fast, just like Mum.

I continued to go to work with mum after school and in the mornings during holiday time. She now had two jobs consisting of three shifts a day, but they were walking distance from home, which was good for her. They were all cleaning jobs, so I used to go with her during holidays. On the morning shift from seven until nine, to help in the kitchen preparing lunches for nurseries. From ten until noon we were cleaning offices, and then, after school, cleaning the nurseries.

This involved everything from sweeping and mopping three very large nursery classrooms, the kitchens, toilets, and dustbins – the lot.

While the staff was there I would sit and read while my mum cleaned. As soon as they left I would take over so my mum could rest. It was hard work, but I loved doing it, it meant Mum could rest, because I knew that, when we got home, she would be busy with the housework. This time was extra special to me as I had my mum to myself, so it was worth all the mopping and cleaning.

We had to be careful though because I was too young to work and if somebody saw me doing it my mum could lose her job. We had already had a warning. On Fridays Mum would give me a few pence and I would skip to the garage and buy a bar of chocolate. Mum would say, 'Eat it before we get home, Pushpa, or your brothers will cry for one as well.'

This made me feel really appreciated. It was as if Mum was saying 'thanks for all the help', but I was glad to help her at work and in our normal daily lives.

I watched my mother work day in day out; she used to get tired so easily that I could not wait to take over from her as soon as the staff left. This way she would rest, I would get to spend this valuable time with her and, of course, I would get 2 pence on Friday. The most enjoyable and memorable moment was holding her hand and feeling it warmly enclosing mine. Gosh, I loved my mother. She was a strong lady to have held so many jobs in one day and kept the household running that had more than fourteen bodies in it.

I admired her courage, because, as with a lot of Asian families that came here in that generation, she could not speak a word of English yet, like them, she was brave enough to go out and find any work that she could just to support the family. My mother joined an English class that was held at the local church once a week. She could not even write her native language, so she was totally illiterate and had to rely on verbal communication to get by, however my father was fluent and would write to his family back home regularly. When my mother wanted to write a letter I would go with her to a lady who lived around the corner from us and she would write the letters we wanted to send and read the ones that we had received. I think Mum did not want my father to see them.

* * * * *

These years were magical for me. I don't know what it was, but I just felt I had to be with Mum as much as possible. I would sneak into her bed at night and sleep curled up at her feet. She would let me have a bath with her, help her to wash the clothes, help in the kitchen, watch her tell my brothers and sister off, even watch her chase brother Ash around the house. This last was because he enjoyed cooking and he would experiment while we were at work. She went berserk because he used to waste so many ingredients, it was so funny, but he didn't understand how hard it was for her to buy those ingredients in the first place.

She would take me wherever she went – or rather I made sure I went with her everywhere I could. That was what my day was like. Mum was my life, my existence; my world revolved around her. I had never imagined that I would, or could, ever be without her, that would be silly and the thought never even crossed my mind.

I think she spent that time with me because I was a girl. My two older sisters were 14 and 13 years older than me and the house was full of boys. I was felt so privileged that I was with her a lot more than some of the others.

My mother was of Asian origin and wore a sari. I would wrap myself in her skirts when she was sitting down. She was very fair in complexion, slightly chubby in a very cute way. She had very rosy cheeks and naturally pink lips. Her eyes were hazel and when she put on the Kajal (eye liner), she looked absolutely stunning.

My father was very strict with her; he did not like her wearing any make-up and would shout even when she had only put some Vaseline on her face. He didn't like her to wear the color red, I don't know why, but I am sure it was because she looked so beautiful in that colour that he was jealous of her. My father was a very proud man and took pride not only in how he looked, but also his family, especially my mum.

My father dressed differently to most men, he used to wear cravats and felt hats. He smoked a pipe, wore only 22 carat buttons on his open neck shirts that were linked with a chain and had a tattoo of a naked women the length of his forearm. He walked with his chest out and hands held behind his back. To this day I have not yet seen anybody dress in this attire as their daily normal dress code. Together my parents made a beautiful couple.

Unfortunately my father had a drinking problem, not continuously, but he would have drinking sessions that lasted for weeks. Then he would be fine again for the same period. I know this problem had started before my dad had married my mother. He also stopped working not long after coming to England because of his drinking. This did not help matters and I know through my elders and what I had witnessed myself that Mum did everything she could possibly do to try and stop him; but nothing worked. My father lost a lot of business in Africa because of his drinking issues.

He would sell my mother's jewellery to buy drink, sober up for a while, make some money and buy it back until it got to a point where he could not afford to retrieve it again. As it was tradition for parents to give their daughters gold bangles and sets of necklaces in their dowries and to give daughter-in-laws gold too, my mother worked the extra shifts so she could put money aside to do this.

So my mother had the running of the household and all the responsibilities of the family. I know that my two elder brothers and sister worked when we came from Africa, so I suppose their contributions helped with the expenses, otherwise how could my mum have fed fourteen mouths and paid all the bills?

So my daily life continued; going to school, going to work and doing whatever I could to help my mum around the house. I felt I was content enough at this point in my life, the days were filled with happiness for me. I played with my brothers, ate my mum's scrumptious cooking, shopped, and visited relatives' houses.

All these memories were surrounded by either hot summer days or snow that fell more than twelve inches! They were awesome times and I never once complained about anything, we were happy with whatever we had and I just loved everything and everyone.

In 1976 my Grandmother - my father's mother – visited from India. My eldest brother Mo, had arranged for her to come, but just before she arrived he moved out, the first to leave the family home.

I spent a lot of time with Grandmother, as mum had asked me to and her visit went by really quickly. She was a lot like my father, quick to make sharp comments. I noticed my mum looking more tired than usual during this period, but she just shrugged it off.

I went on a visit to my eldest sister Ursula's in Preston in November that year. I had not wanted to go, I don't know what it was, but I did not want to leave my mum behind.

While I was at my sister's home the phone rang one evening. It was Mo telling us that my mum was not well. I wanted to go home right away, but Mo said 'No, don't come back, she'll be fine. Just finish your holiday.'

I did everything I could to persuade my sister to let us go back, but it was two days later before we finally left. The four-hour trip back home seemed never-ending and I remember a feeling of panic inside as I sat in the back of the car. Why weren't we there yet? Why was it taking so long?

My usual travel sickness did not even cross my mind; all I could think about was Mum.

At last we pulled up outside our house and I was out of the car almost before it had stopped. I ran to my mum in the kitchen; she looked withdrawn and had dark circles around her eyes. I was just so relieved to be at home with her I didn't really think about it, I was back with my mum, so I was happy.

The days went by and the time came for my Grandmother to go back to India. Her visit had been a real strain on Mum, so I was secretly pleased that she was going.

Mum looked more ill everyday. I still have a photo of us together at Diwali; how tired she looked in her pink sari. I had visited the doctor with her, but was still too young to really understand what was going on. Then she had to go into hospital. The day she went in I remember thinking 'How will I get through the day and who will comb my hair.' With the self-absorbed focus of a child I just wanted my mum to come home. Nobody told me why she was in hospital.

I don't remember much about the next few months; I remember visiting my mum in hospital after school, but not much else. I just wanted to be with Mum and spent as much time as I was allowed with her.

She looked pale and sad; I know she was making herself more ill thinking about us at home and worrying. I wanted to tell her not to worry; just to get better. My heart cried for her silently each moment, whether I was with her or away from her. I urged her to get better and come home so that we could all be together again.

On the way to school I walked past the hospital. I felt sad to think my mum was in there all alone. I didn't want to go to school, I wanted to stay with her. My mum was far more important than school and I resented everybody that told me to go to school. A couple of months down the line, when I went to visit mum, I saw my father beside her, he was always at the hospital which I thought was amazing and felt really proud of him because he just loved her so much and it was so evident to the eye.

I used to think that if I am going through this awful pain then how much my dad must be hurting. He was a very proud man and did not show his emotions well, but his eyes expressed his pain.

Mum was really ill. One day I walked down the ward towards her bed and gasped in horror. She was holding a cardboard tray beneath her face and blood was gushing from her nose into it. She'd had a blood transfusion, but her body wouldn't accept it. I cried and could not take my eyes off her. How did it get this bad? This image has stayed with me ever since. It was difficult to understand what all the doctors and my elders were saying about her illness, I just wished that I had the ability to stop her suffering and bring her back home. I needed her.

Finally Mum was allowed to come home for two weeks. She was just skin and bones and looked very weak, but she was home and that was all that mattered. I bathed her with my sister, using a sponge and bucket. She had to sleep downstairs, because she was too weak to walk.

I promised myself that, as soon as she was back to normal and we returned to work, I would do most of the cleaning so she could rest more and not become ill again.

The fortnight went by too quickly, and before we knew it she was back in hospital. The hospital knew something that we did not and that's why they allowed her home, but I didn't know that then. I was simply very grateful to have my mum at home for a while and couldn't wait till she came home again.

My mother passed away on 15th June 1977.

The last time I saw my mum alive, she was fighting to stay alive. Her eyes and skin had gone pale and white, I remember the doctors saying it was because of the medication and they told us to go home and let her rest.

My father and elder brothers came home and told us. I sat on the floor watching my dad and thinking, 'When am I going to be able to talk to her again?'

My father said, 'She didn't want to die. She was scared to leave us all behind. She was only worried that she had not yet had the bangles made for your dowry, Pushpa. She made us promise to do that for you.' And my father had to stop. He left the room abruptly.

Over the next few days it seemed as though hundreds of people were in the house. The twelve-day mourning period was horrible, but I suppose it was good that we weren't on our own and did not wallow in our loss. At night I cried silently in my room, when my sister came to bed she was crying too. I turned around and put my arms around her back to console her and we cried together until we fell asleep.

The mourning days went by in a haze. The whole thing was crazy in my eyes; we had so many people coming to our house during those twelve days, people that we did not even know. They would bring food for us because we were not allowed to light the gas in our house until after the final ceremony on the final day. Some of the food was inedible – it tasted nothing like my mum's cooking, but we were grateful that they were bringing it for us. At least it made us laugh having to eat the same lentil curry for a few days cooked by different people. The expressions on my brothers' faces as they ate said it all.

It was very strange; we were supposed to be sad all the time, but odd things kept happening, which would make us, smile. I think my mum made it so we did not cry all the time. However, on the day of the funeral and the final day of mourning I could not stop myself and cried uncontrollably. The priest told us that this final twelfth day was the day that the soul leaves us for good and we would have no ties with mum from then on; we had to let her go.

The day of the funeral was chaotic. The coffin was covered in purple velvet – my favorite colour and I wondered who had picked this colour. The twelve of us stood around the coffin, I was at my mum's feet. When I looked at her face she had gone back to look as she did before she became ill; she looked radiant. They had dressed her as a bride, in red; she was so beautiful. I looked at her feet; she had red sandals on and her nails were painted for the first time that I had ever seen. I thought, 'I will never sleep at your feet again'. I put my hand out to touch her toes, they were cold.

The ceremony started and my father had to do everything. I watched his every move; he never once cried and did everything perfectly.

We all had to walk around my mum several times I looked at her every part to memorize how beautiful and perfect she was, her hands, her lips. Her hair was very dry; she did not have the oil in it that she used each day in her hair as well as mine. She looked very young, but she was, oh, my God, my mother was only 42 years old. Why would God want to take her at such a young age?

I had planned to look after her when I got older, I wanted to be with her all my life and would never have let her struggle ever, why did God not let her live to see these days of happiness that her twelve children would have given her. Why did he not leave her here with us, why had he taken this opportunity away from us, from me and the promise I had made to look after her, why?

I don't recall what I was feeling during the ceremony, it was as if I had gone numb. I looked around and saw my elders crying. I think my younger brothers were as numb as I was.

When it came to closing the coffin, I felt as if something exploded within me and I screamed, I looked at my mother's face, it was covered in red powder from the ceremony I almost cried out 'Please don't go'.

When my father and brothers carried the coffin out I clung on to my brother Will and looked into his eyes and said, 'Stop, please stop', begging him not to take Mum. He cried and shook his head, then somebody grabbed me from behind and said, 'Let her go.' They started to chant Hare Krishna in my ears to calm me down. I watched the coffin go, my hand was on the hearse as it drove away. Oh, my God where was my mum going?

When everybody returned from the crematorium I ran to the door to let them in, but was told by others that they could not step over the door until they had had a wash and changed their clothes. That was silly, I thought, as all I wanted to do was hug my brother and my father. The women were not allowed to go to the crematorium according to tradition, nobody explained why. A few moments later I saw my father in the garden throwing a bucket of water on himself, another tradition to bathe in the clothes that were worn at the funeral. I felt for him so much, he looked so alone, yet so brave. I had not yet seen him shed a tear.

My mother's ashes were sent to India to my Father's brother, who in turn arranged for them to be scattered in the cleanest part of the river Ganges at the bottom of the Himalayas in Haridwar, north of India.

This was the closure of my first door and this is my traumatic yet amazing journey. From the day I lost my mother my life had turned completely, from being a child to becoming an adult overnight having to make life-impacting decisions. Being afraid yet carrying on, missing the opportunities, doing things so others did not do without and living life as I thought was expected of me.

TWO

Unlocking The Door

Growing up for me was a mixture of sadness, adventure, being a child, being mature and so much more than a normal child of my age would probably have experienced. I know that all that had happened in my early years has in some way directed me to be the person that I am today. From living a meaningless and sad life for many years I am now a grateful individual for my many journeys through life to where I am today.

I remember so well my feelings when my mother passed away, I really needed the comfort of a hug from any of the women in the family. They had never said that, although my mother was not around anymore, they would be there for me. These women were all at least a dozen years older than me and were in my immediate family, but couldn't see how much I needed them and their support.

I just took it on board and knew that I was expected to carry on my own. My sister Ursula was good over the phone; when I was struggling with cooking I would call her for advice on how to do things, but it was awkard as she was so far away.

Most of the time that I was with my brothers was fantastic as my mind was occupied with them or with the other chores. I suppose thinking about it now, that taking on the responsibilities and making the decision to do all and run the household had probably been a good idea as it kept my mind occupied, so I didn't dwell on the things I did not have. When I came home at least I was not hanging about watching television and or simply passing the time. I didn't have time to brood over my situation, it was a matter of getting changed and just getting on with what I had to do.

The lonely times came when I was in my bedroom alone. We had a town house that had four very large bedrooms, two reception rooms, a dining room, a kitchen and a large back garden with apple and pear trees. My mother used to plant herbs, garlic and all sorts in the garden. There was one room for the girls and my brothers and parents were divided in the rest. This was when my mother was alive.

The elder brothers occupied the two top rooms with their wives until they moved out. My sisters and I shared a room on the second floor, next to my parents and five brothers and then two brothers occupied one of the reception rooms downstairs.

When the house was full it was amazing as my mum's room was next to mine. It made it easier for me to sneak into her room at night and sleep by her feet. I loved sleeping there, the scent of her and the touch of her feet was so comforting. I think that because my mum had to divide her attention between so many of us I made the most of the moments that I could be with her.

When both sisters married, the room became my own and when my 2 elder brothers moved out the younger brothers spread themselves out in the house. My bedroom used to be daunting at times. When I was in there I would be constantly revisiting the past and visualising the future. I cried a lot in that room and talked a lot to an imaginary person, really it was my mother. I sometimes thought I was going mad, but then thought again and knew it was good that I was letting my emotions go. This let me get on with my normal life and be happy as the days went by.

This got into a habit, which I have practiced all my life. If I feel I need to talk to somebody or am overwhelmed with emotion I will go to the quiet of my room, have a good chat with that imaginary listener, have a good cry, go back to the others and get on with what I have to as if nothing was any different.

When my brother Dev decided he was going to get married, my initial thought was a selfish one. I thought that he and his wife would stay with us at my father's house for a while, as was the Asian tradition in those days. I thought, 'Wow; it is going to be really great to have another female in the house.' I could be all girly again, but most of all I was looking for the companionship.

But this was not to be. My brother had already bought his house, to which we all contributed to make it awesome for him to live in and he had already decided that he was going to start living there immediately after the wedding.

I think he was also concerned that my father had drinking bouts, which would be uncomfortable for his wife. I told myself it would be OK, I was used to living my way and was sure that in the near future something else or someone would come along.

I still had my friend too. It was a funny friendship, we hadn't really become friends until we were fourteen years old. We hardly ever used to meet, but would write to each other and make the odd phone call.

Today she is still that one friend that I have and the relationship still follows the same form. We hardly ever meet, even once year would be lucky, but we try and call each other once in while, even if it is just to exchange comments about the weather or something silly. We provide words of encouragement to each other and anything else that needs talking about. It is weird but today I know that she was and is my true friend and even though we never make that many physical meetings happen I know that, if ever the need arose, I could count on her to be there and vice versa.

When things were really bad for me and I managed to get a hold of her via the phone, I would blurt out whatever I needed to get off my chest and share my enormous issues. It has always been calming just to hear her words of reassurance.

So, life went on. One thing that I was so grateful for was that we had to wear uniforms at school. The coat and shoes my mother had bought me lasted for years; she had always bought things a couple of sizes bigger than needed. We were also lucky in the first two years that we were given a grant for our uniforms and shoes and also free lunches because my father was a single parent. This helped the family finances now my mum was not there to earn the money to provide all the things she had done.

My brothers did well to make their clothes last and, as Dev was working and, eventually, Shiv started, their contributions helped. Money was not an issue with us, yes, it would have been good to have more, maybe to buy a car, and not have to budget for everything. Yes, it would have been nice to be able to buy better food, furniture or clothes, but we had never had these luxuries so we did not know what we were missing. We got by, although even now I sometimes wonder how.

It was an incredible journey for us but we made up for the sad times by just larking around and having a laugh. We did a lot of that and, to this day, my brothers and I seem to talk only of the fun times. The cheapest food or the smallest gift we bought each other was appreciated so much and treasured as though it was the most important thing we had.

I liked to think that my mum was watching us and that she was very proud of the way we were all surviving. I wondered how she was feeling, because she was not here with us. I cannot even begin to think about what she must have been going through knowing she was about to leave us all behind.

I never really saw myself as a girl until much later on in life and never ever pampered myself with make up and girly things. Although I did dream, I dreamed that boys would be interested in me, that I would have wonderful clothes and be able to go shopping with my friends and buy the latest clothes, shoes and magazines. I wanted to be like them, to wear make-up, to have long hair, I wanted my parents to come to parents evening like the others did. I wanted a normal childhood.

I wanted to be dropped off at school instead of walking every day I wanted to say 'goodbye' to my mum in the morning. I knew I was wasting my time wanting all these things, so I replaced these dreams with others.

I wanted the best for my brothers, the best food and clothes I could give them. My youngest brother, Chandan, did not even know how to tie his shoe laces, one of us had to do it for him. He was still a baby really and was our responsibility.

I felt for my brothers and their loss too. I also saw that they really coped well. I wondered if they also cried quietly when they were alone, as I did.

I decided to give up studying. I was struggling to retain knowledge with all that was going on around me. We needed the additional income.

Getting a job was hard at the beginning, I lost the little contact I had with my school friends who went on to study through university. I became more of a loner, going to work and coming straight home to do whatever was needed. I avoided making friends at work in case they demanded my time; I just didn't have enough time to go to the cinemas or clubs, or even shopping.

But life had to go on. After my mum's funeral we rarely had any visits from the relatives that used to come when my mum was around. The people that did come were from the church where we used to go to Sunday school. These were the people we had met at bible classes before my mum died. It was good to have them there, just for the company and encouragement. They did not make us feel like outcasts as a lot of others did.

I learnt to cook, clean, run the household and do the shopping. My brothers used to help a lot, I used to write down chores on pieces of papers and we had to pick them out, then it was up to the individual to do that chore for the week. Chores included cleaning the bathrooms, vacuuming, mopping, cleaning out the gutter, helping to cook meals and everything else a household needed to continue to function. It was fun and Manish usually nearly always got to clean the gutters and the toilets.

Shiv opted to make the chapattis (bread) to eat with our food everyday. I think he hated the task and would make them first thing in the morning to get the task out of the way! I remember when my mum was around and my elder sisters used to make them; they made a huge pile every day because there were sixteen people in the family to feed. I think eventually they started resenting that they had to do it every day, but, hey, it was expected of them to be able to cook before they married, so that they would get good husbands and in-laws.

They are supposed to be nice and round, but Shiv's efforts came in all shapes and sizes. Some were shaped like a map of United Kingdom! At dinner time we would laugh at the shapes, put them in the middle of the table and spin them, wherever the thinnest point pointed that person had to eat that one. They sometimes used to be really hard to chew and I used to watch my father struggle to eat them at all. He complained now and again because of his teeth, so I used to ensure that he had the softest one. We were really grateful to have food on our table and I was just glad that my brother made them for us so that I did not have to make them every day.

My brothers were truly good. I remember the first time I cooked it was a lentil curry – it tasted disgusting! Perhaps I didn't wash it properly or put too much of a certain spice in it. I made a huge pot like my mum used to cook in. Nobody complained, not even my father.

The next day I put lots of sugar and yogurt in it to disguise the flavour; they still ate it without complaining. My cooking improved as the years went by; I always tasted it to ensure it tasted similar to my mum's. I learnt to cook so many dishes and I remember the church people complimenting me on my food, it was amazing. If I wanted to make something and was unsure I would call my sister Ursula and ask her the ingredients and how to make it. Even she thought my cooking was excellent.

It got to point that whenever my sisters and their families, or anybody else came around I would have food prepared and also used to make the spices like my mum used to and pack some to give to them the same way she did. I felt as if some force guided my hand, it was absolutely amazing. Ash (the one my mum used to chase because he was always in the kitchen experimenting) was awesome. He cooked some amazing dishes using cookbooks and always came shopping with me as well. Most of the time though, I used to drag all of them down to the shops. We would visit different shops for different things, there was the local shop for all our Asian groceries, then the superstore for the routine day-to-day things and the fish and meat shops. I learned to cook traditional Asian dishes instead of settling for easier options, I really wanted to keep things going the way my mother had.

My shopping list was the same every week and I would put the same amount of money aside for all the things such as bills, food, spending money and so on. We never had a lot of money, I used to get family allowance from my father, who would first take out his drink and tobacco money and give me the rest. My father would have some money to buy any particular food that he fancied during the week for he was also an excellent cook.

During the time when my mum was ill, he had cooked the meals and had managed to set the fridge on fire. It was funny, but his cooking was out of this world and I was really glad that he had considered Mum by letting her rest. He would buy his fish, or whatever, and cook it for himself. Sometimes we would have some as well.

I also used to get contributions from the brothers that worked, which helped. With a limited budget we used to have the same food every day of the week, it made it easier for me to prepare before going school, except on Saturday nights when we treated ourselves. Saturday nights were special – we might have samosas, or stuffed parathas or some other treat we would look forward to all week.

Saturday lunch was always the same was according to what my father wanted; a yogurt curry, rice with lentils, lentils made with salt and a little spice and sweet semolina.

Once that was over my brothers and I would prepare the evening meal and had so much fun doing it. Although we didn't eat luxuriously, we enjoyed what we had. We looked forward to Saturdays as we spent the afternoon together preparing the evening meal; because of this my brothers are excellent in preparing foods and cooking. Will is so like my father in his cooking and watching him cook is like watching my father. They both love to cook and then to sit back and watch us enjoy the meals they had created. During these times I knew in my heart that my mum was still with us.

Dev helped me with paying the bills and running things around the house for a while, but then he had planned to get married and had bought his own place, so that was one less contribution. We missed him immensely, he was the most serious of us all, but also to me he was the most supportive and always had faith and respected the decisions I made while looking after the home. Taking on my mother's role made me more mature and responsible. I grew up much sooner than I would have done had my mum been around.

It was after my 16th birthday that I knew I could not continue with my studies. I made my decision to leave college for a while and let my other brothers finish their education first. Lalita had come to stay with us while her husband was abroad. It was good to have her and her baby daughter with us. I used to drop my little niece off at the babysitters in the morning and pick her up on the way back from college, she was really cute, and I built an extra-special bond with her. When she was ill in hospital I stayed with her, we were very close – and still are to this day.

With the help of my Ash's girlfriend I was able to get a job in a factory. I had worked in an engineering factory during the summer with Will, but this was my first 'real' job. This job was part clerical administration and if the need arose I would be required to work on the factory floor. I was getting paid £55.00 a week, which made a big difference to the family income. I was even able to buy some new clothes to wear to work and also bought some clothes for my brothers.

I started to have driving lessons with somebody that we knew. He gave me a special deal, as I was his first student in our town.

Within a few months I was promoted to be a payroll and admin clerk. This meant that I was full time in the offices and did not need to work on the machines on the factory floor. Soon the company opened a new warehouse and I got promoted to a financial administration role. By this time I was on £69.00 a week. I never praised myself; I just thought it was good luck. If people told me I was doing a brilliant job, I would brush it off. I could not accept the fact that I was any good, I don't know what it was, but I always felt that people looked down on me.

It was the same with everything; if ever anybody gave me anything I would feel guilty for taking it, while in mind I am racking my brain for things that I could give back in return and would give them double back even if I could not afford to and it meant me doing without. I think a lot of people realised this. I was to learn later on in life that some people really did not care about me, but were just interested in what I could give or do for them.

I loved people visiting us and I would do anything to make them feel welcome in our home. They loved my cooking, but we often found ourselves looking after their children and doing many other things.

When I think about it today, I realise I was looking for approval from others. I don't know why, maybe it was the constant insecurity I felt within me. But if someone said to me they really liked something I did, I was really pleased that they had enjoyed it and would already be thinking of what else I could do for them. Once I have made a commitment I will carry the action through no matter what the situation.

Even though I had all these people coming around me to visit or eat or anything, I still felt so alone and sorry for myself, but I kept that to myself.

So life carried on for me, I was working, no pressure of studies any more and becoming an amazing housekeeper and a brilliant cook in the process. My brothers did well, too, and I used to think that whomever they married would be lucky women. My brothers cleaned and cooked brilliantly now, like it was second nature to them.

My father continued to have drinking sessions, but now that we were much older and experienced, we were able to handle the situation more efficiently.

My six brothers and I were a team and we did brilliantly. I still cried every night for Mum, yet I would always fall asleep on the thought that, one day, I will have somebody to love and care for me in this physical world as much as I would for them. My only regret was that mum would not be there to see this happening, or to tell me whether I was doing the right thing or not.

I remember my father telling me once that he had promised my mother that he would never leave us, be it through death or going to India or re-marrying or for any other reason. He had made a promise to my mother that he would stay with us until I had got married and was settled. That was what she was worried about when she was in hospital. Mum had asked him for assurance, and, of course, the gold bangles for my dowry would be made for me.

This made me think that I would love to get married eventually, now that mum was not here for me to look after. I would find my prince who would to look after me, have the perfect wedding day and make my parents very proud. In the Asian tradition it was very important for us to get married within the caste and, typically, live with our in-laws abiding by all their rules and living to their standards. I knew I would do this the best I could, so Mum and Dad would be proud.

Then it happened. That summer I met my prince; the man who would become my husband. It was at a friend's house, a girl that I had built up a friendship with. This friendship happened when we were really young and our mothers worked together in the town. Her family then moved away and I did not see her again till I was fourteen. We did not go to each other's house that often but would write to each other weekly, even though we only lived about half an hour or so apart. I preferred to stay at home and I looked forward to reading and writing the letters. I could talk about other things away from the home environment and would also make up fictitious stories about the things I wished for in life.

I don't know what it was but I felt safer writing my dreams on paper rather than talking about it. She was my only and best friend, her mother was awesome, but was always telling me that I should marry soon and have a different life to the one I was living currently. She used to tell me that I deserved to be happy and she knew I would give only the best to whoever became my partner.

As I never left my house other than to go shopping or town with my brothers and of course I had no social life, I thought that meeting somebody was going to be impossible. I reckoned without my family, my sisters and others were fully focused on setting me up for an arranged marriage. Urgh! I could not even begin to imagine what it would be like to marry someone I didn't know. I knew that arranged marriages did work, but that wasn't what I wanted.

I did like boys, but I felt I was not attractive to them. There was one boy I had liked since we were eleven, right up to being sixteen. I had never spoken to him, but having the opportunity to just daydream was enough to keep me happy. I dreamed that maybe one day he would speak to me. It's amazing when I look back and think that the possibility of this happening over six years had kept me daring to dream of a fantastic life, especially when you consider my situation at that time.

Nothing ever did come of this, I never spoke to that boy although I still wonder what he is doing now. He is almost certainly a professional somewhere, because he was the most intellectual boy in our year with close to 100% pass rates in all the subjects. I admired him because he was in the position where I would have loved to be during my time at school and college.

I saw another young man at my sister's wedding, and again kept hoping, waiting for something to happen, too afraid to speak to him. It was another daydream that kept me going. I looked forward to any occasion at which I thought he would be. You know how it is, you live in anticipation and excitement just in case you bump into the guy, which did not happen very often. I noticed he was wonderful with his family and was always considerate of others, I know that was what had really attracted me to him.

He was a vegetarian, was in the same caste, did not drink alcohol, had a decent job and was very sensible. When my family was trying to arrange a marriage meeting with some guy that I had not even heard of, I dropped his name into the conversation. My sister and brothers thought it was a wonderful idea, so they approached his family with this suggestion. Unfortunately his father was very strict and said no, because apparently his family were from the same village in India as my grandmother. I don't think we were blood related at all, but had called him 'uncle' out of respect from way back.

So that was the end of that dream! Once again it looked as though the door of life was firmly shut again. I was grasping for any possibility of ever having a life like other girls my age had. I did pretend I had it all – why not? I would, tell myself that lots of people pretend, so why shouldn't I?

I visualised that my father was happy, that Mum was back with us, that my brothers were educated and had settled and I was the happiest person in the world with the most amazing soul mate giving me more care and love than you could possibly imagine. There was no harm in dreaming if it gave you the strength to face each day with something to look forward to.

Anyway, let's get back to how I met my husband. My friend's mother (or aunty as I called her) rang and asked me to come and help her to do some cooking, as she was expecting some guests. I was busy myself, but told her I would come as soon as I could.

I went after lunch on a Sunday in my jeans and t-shirt. When I got there she told me that my friend had gone away for the day. I suggested that we get started immediately on the preparation, as I needed to be home soon.

To get to the kitchen I had to go through the back room, as I opened the door I saw this guy sitting on the sofa having a drink. Aunty came up behind me and introduced us. Frankly, I was suspicious of her innocent tactics, as this was the second person she had introduced me to in the same number of months. I did not look at him for more than a couple of seconds, as usual, I became very self-conscious, said 'hello' and dashed into the kitchen. Aunty then told me that her friends were not coming and suggested we went and joined him for a while. She also said he was the son of her late husband's niece.

Yes, I thought, she was up to her tricks again, but found it really amusing and couldn't help, but laugh at what she was trying to do and, of course, she had called me today knowing full well that my friend was away. But she did apologise for having made me come all that way and insisted that I to have at least one drink before I headed back home. 'OK', I said, helping myself to some juice.

I went back to the room and took a close look at the guy sitting down. He looked rugged, had a beard and was wearing a light blue checked shirt and jeans. I caught his eye and lingered for a moment, I had seen him somewhere before, but I couldn't place where from immediately.

I went and stood by the window and aunty started talking. I wasn't really listening, I was racking my brain to remember where I had seen him before.

No good, I didn't have a clue. Aunty made some excuse and left the room for a moment, that's when he spoke.

'Who is your father?' he asked.

My tongue was in a knot as I mumbled the answer. I felt very conscious of my cropped hair style, not the usually accepted style for girls like me.

'Are you still at college?' he asked.

'Er, no,' I said. 'I'm having a break; I have family commitments right now. Although I'd like to go back and continue my studies.'

'Are you working, then?' he asked.

We were having a full-blown conversation! We talked about where I worked, how long I had been there and so on, and I told him briefly what I did.

The conversation only lasted a few minutes. Considering I had never really spoken to anybody in that context for any length of time before, I was feeling quite pleased with myself. I was still uncomfortable though, my voice was shaky, and so I picked up my glass and told him I had to go.

I went to the front room and told my aunt that I was leaving. She didn't say much, but nodded her head. I understood that she was asking me if I liked the man. I shook my head vigorously to say 'no way'.

I said goodbye and she told me to call her as soon as I had reached home safely

As I left I thought 'oh, my God! How embarrassing. However I couldn't stop myself from smiling, at least I got through the experience, but it felt more like an interview than a conversation. I guessed that this was the process that young people go through when marriages were arranged. I also realised that I was not defensive as usual when it came to talking to him. In my normal daily life I would say the words that people expected me to say and not really say what I was truly feeling. You could say I was not being true to myself, but at that point in my life I knew no better.

As I walked up a very steep hill thinking about how this had been a waste of my time when I had so much to do at home, it clicked in my head where I had seen him before, it was at his sister's wedding about two years ago, his name was Chandra, but was known as Jimmy to almost all who knew him.

I remembered the day exactly, I had worn a maroon sari and had made an effort to look pretty, I don't know why, but, hey, it was a wedding after all. We were with the groom's side of the family I knew that my friend was going to be there and we had planned what we were going to wear.

Lunch was served in the usual style as a buffet where we could all help ourselves. As I was standing in the queue I noticed my cousin's brother serving and said hello to him,. I moved to the next dish and said 'yes please' to the young man who was serving and looked up at him to say 'thanks'. He was very tall and my eyes travelled upwards. Our eyes met and he had the most amazing eyes, which mesmerised me. He had a cheeky sort of grin on his face. 'Er, thanks,' I said. He grinned back.

I didn't realise he was the bride's brother, as he was not wearing a suit or tie. I carried on walking down the line and every time I looked back I saw him watching me. My stomach felt as though a platoon of butterflies were doing aerobatics in there!

It was only when they were taking the family photos that I realised that he was the bride's brother. Soon after that we left and I forgot about the incident.

On the Tuesday following my aunt's matchmaking efforts, I left the office and started to walk towards the bus stop. Half way down the street there was a man in the distance coming towards me with a suitcase in his hand. I just looked down and carried on walking, I then heard someone say 'Hi!'

I looked up. It was him! I remember thinking 'Oh my God, what is he doing here?' What was I going to do now?

I said 'Hi!' back to him and continued to walk. He swung into step and walked beside me

'Is this where you work?' he asked, nodding at the building I'd just left.

'Yes,' I said. 'What are you doing in this area, I haven't seen you around here before?'

'Oh, I thought you would like to accompany me to the coach station, seeing as it is on your way home.'

I was dumbfounded, thinking what an idiot, why come all the way across town past the station in the first instance to ask me to walk back with him. A crazy guy, I thought.

'I need to catch the bus,' I said.

'That's OK,' he answered cheerfully. We continued to walk in silence towards the bus stop.

The bus came and he followed me onto it. We went into town with my heart beating furiously. I was continually aware of the people around us and was terrified that someone who knew me would see us and tell my father what I was up to.

For God's sake, I told myself, you are only going into town like you do every day. I thought that I would leave me at the coach station, what was the harm in that and, anyway, nobody would see us.

When we got to the station, he asked me to sit with him there for a while until my bus came; we were just talking generally about my work and his family business. I was still very conscious of people walking by and still fearful in case anybody saw us.

Jimmy told me he was going to London and asked if he could have my phone number so that he could call me sometime, I was hesitant and still couldn't see why he would want to call me.

He was really handsome and had a really unique grin and an air of laughter about him. It really was impossible not to smile when you saw him or heard him speak. I gave in and gave him the number.

'I really have to get home,' I said, feeling more and more flustered.

'Yes, I suppose you do,' he said. 'We'll talk again soon.'

I flushed as I said goodbye. I was still in shock on the way home, not believing what had happened. I still could not understand why he came all the way to my work place just to ask me to see him off at the coach station.

How weird was that, I thought!

THREE

Stepping Through The Door

I could not get him off my mind all the way home and kept smiling at the cheek of it. At that time I was so naïve that I still hadn't realised that he had come to see me intentionally. Why would he do that for a girl that looked like a tomboy? Even my father used to get angry with me sometimes, because he thought he had been talking to my brother and I would correct him by telling him it was I. He would then have a go at me for having cut my hair so short so I that he could not tell the difference. I didn't wear any makeup and made no effort whatsoever to make myself look good or feminine.

Once I got home, I soon forgot about the incident as I got on with the housework and cooking as my sister Ursula and her family had arrived for a fasting festival.

We were having a small barbeque in the garden before the fast started and although I did hear the phone ring, which it had done several times, I did not run to answer it. I knew my brothers would, when my brother Govind came round the back and said somebody kept calling and putting the receiver down as soon as he had said 'hello', I did not think much of it.

When the barbeque was finished, we settled down to watch television and the phone rang again. I went to answer it while my eyes were still on the screen. Until recently we had a coin box telephone, to ensure that we didn't run up a big phone bill that we would not be able to pay. This also meant that neighbours could use it just like a telephone booth. However, we'd recently changed the phone from a coin box to a normal phone. There was a little hatch between the two reception rooms where we had put the telephone, so the phone could be answered from both rooms and, of course, everybody could hear the conversations.

I said 'hello', and the person on the end said 'hello'.

'Who is this?' I asked.

'It's me,' came the reply.

I thought it was one of my brothers' friends messing around and said 'Who's me?'

'It's Jim, I'm still on my way to London, but we've stopped at a service station for a break. I just wanted to make sure you got home OK.'

I felt my cheeks flush and my stomach churned. He sounded really different on the phone; more husky and older. I was really surprised that he had called and realising that he had tried several times surprised me even more.

At first I was tongue tied, I didn't know what to say. My family was sitting around me and I was very aware that they would hear every word I said. It was the first time somebody had actually called me - and it was a shock. My brain was not connecting with my mouth and I was finding it really difficult to come out with anything sensible.

'I'll call you tomorrow, if that's okay. Will you answer the phone if I call at 10.00pm?' he said.

I thought this was late and knew it would be difficult with my father sleeping in the room directly above, but I couldn't say that. 'Yes, OK,' I said instead.

I would just have to wait and see what happened when he rang. I was frightened and excited all at once. It couldn't be all that bad; it was only a telephone call, after all. Somehow 'only a telephone call' had an unnerving effect on me, though; I definitely could not get him off my mind! My mind and feelings were all over the place.

This was the first time I had ever in my life spoken to a male who wasn't a family member or a friend of my family. This was different – he was talking to me, because he wanted to, not because he was being polite. This realisation made me feel shaky inside. When we had met on Sunday at Aunt's house, I may have denied that I was at all interested in him, but, wow, my emotions were all over the place and I was totally confused about what to do next.

I put the phone down and knew that I could not go dancing around the house shouting about what had just happened, no matter how much I might have felt like it. I just kept my mouth shut and acted as if nothing was going on yet my insides were in turmoil; could one phone call actually do this to a person?

Apart from my close family, nobody had ever been interested in whether I was okay. I'd never had a boy show any interest in me. It was scary and felt weird; I had always appeared to be independent and strong. I was the one who looked after others, so it was hard to accept somebody being nice to me.

Since my mother had died I'd put a shield on my feelings. I didn't express love or happiness, everything was under control. I told myself that if I didn't feel then I wouldn't hurt. That's how I got through my days, it was what kept me going for years. My friend had once told me that it was impossible to close your heart and yet still love some people. You either loved or not; there were no in-between – and I loved my family and close friends so I hadn't lost the ability, I simply hadn't been in this situation before.

I still dreamed of becoming a professional and being married to somebody who would give me the life full of happiness and fun, but I'd never thought about how that would happen or what I would need to do to achieve these dreams.

Obviously I had to study to get the qualifications I needed to enter any profession. Somewhere I had a vague feeling that, once I was qualified, I would be someone and it would be easy to meet the right person. I never dreamt that I would have the courage to do it. I also didn't want to do anything that would tarnish my parent's reputation and knew that, if I took any steps towards my dreams, it would be according to tradition as expected by my family.

I went to bed, but spent the night tossing and turning. Why had he called or come to see me? What might happen next, especially if my father found out? I was thinking into the future, a million thoughts were going around in my head. I dared not tell anybody at home, but was sure they would notice immediately.

The next day I went to work still not feeling quite right and wishing it was 10pm. The day crawled by and I had no idea what I was doing for most of it. I got home, cooked dinner and sat down with the family to watch television after we had eaten. I claimed the chair beside the piano – and the telephone!

Everybody else was watching the television when the phone rang.

'Hello,' I said.

'Hello. Can you talk?' he asked.

'Not really,' I responded, scared he would ring off and never ring back.

'Are you all right?' he asked.

'Oh, yes,' I reassured him – although I felt anything but 'all right', my stomach was turning somersaults.

He told me a bit about what he was doing in London, that he was probably going to be there for a few weeks and then asked 'Is it okay for me to call you again during the week?'

'Yes,' I said. And we said goodbye.

I hung up and then kicked myself for hardly saying anything other than 'yes' and 'no'. Then I realised - oh no, I hadn't asked him which day he would ring. I would just have to sit by the phone each day to ensure that I answered it. I guessed that he would probably call about the same time.

Then I started thinking, maybe I didn't have to answer it. I could ignore it; maybe that way he would not call again. But I knew I wanted to hear his voice again, he had a tone that made you want to just listen forever.

'What are you going on about, you idiot,' I said to myself, 'you are not supposed to be thinking like that and this is definitely not supposed to be happening!' But it was.

He called several times after that, I didn't have to wait long to grab the phone before anyone else got near it. We talked about what he had done during the day and what I had done. He always asked me what I had cooked, so I guessed he loved his food. I discovered that his parents were really good cooks, in fact his mother had cooked at my sister 2's wedding when I was seven years old.

He appeared to be quite macho to me, mature in his talk, confident and he knew what he was talking about. I loved to hear him laugh, it made me smile, so I would try to talk about things that would make him laugh.

He was diplomatic, and used humour to ensure nobody was upset. For example he commented on my brothers being 'geeks', because they all wore glasses, but then added a comment to it so I wasn't offended. He talked about my father with nothing other than utmost respect, never once did he comment on his drinking issues, which I was really grateful for I knew the whole of our community was aware of the situation; he must have known.

About a week later he asked me if I would like to come down to London for a day. This was another new experience – and I did not know what to do.

I knew it would be wrong, as I would have to make up some excuse to tell my father about where I was going and would have to take a day off work. As my friend (aunt's daughter) was totally unaware of what was happening so I couldn't enlist her help. I needed advice and finally spoke to my brother. He suggested that I go, but warned me to be careful and to be back home at the usual time as if it was a normal working day.

As I booked the tickets I was still unsure of whether I was doing the right thing, but something inside me kept pushing me. I went ahead, took the first step and opened up a new door in my life. Daring to do something that was against all my beliefs, and those of my father, was a turning point in my life.

On the day I was really nervous, I wore a white blouse and a sky blue skirt to match the sky as it was a beautiful sunny hot. I loved the hot weather.

At last the train drew into London. I picked up my bag, smoothed my skirt and stood up. I followed the crowd along the platform and suddenly there was a gap in the crowd and I saw him standing at the end of the platform. He really did look rather scruffy with his beard and the casual way he stood; I liked it. I sighed with relief that he was there and smiled at him. Anybody that looked at this guy had to smile it was just something about him, he smiled back and I felt something deep move inside me.

'Hi,' he said with a grin.

'Hi,' I answered. We fell into step and walked out of the station.

The day went by in a flash. It was my first experience being in London, the first time I'd travelled on my own, and my first date! We walked on bridges, across the River Thames, past the Parliament and Big Ben and ended up on a boat for a drink.

The talk was casual and I let him do most of it, I loved listening to his voice it had so much charisma! It never occurred to me that this effect was simply chemistry – I thought he did this to everyone. As we had walked I noticed how much taller he was, at least a foot taller than me. It made me feel safe and protected.

I did not really want to leave him, and felt sad when we reached the station. Jim came to the platform and put his hand on my back as I climbed onto the train. This was the first time since I met him that we had had any physical contact, he'd always been a real gentleman from the start. It was a light touch like a feather, rather than a heavy hand.

We said our goodbyes and he told me that he would call later to ensure I had reached home safely. My heart felt heavy, yet I still wouldn't admit how my feelings for him had grown in such a short space of time.

A fortnight later the phone calls stopped. There was no warning, no indication that he would not call again. They just stopped. I was devastated and racked my brains as to what I might have said.

I had survived all these years by enclosing my heart in stone, so that I did not have to feel and could not hurt. I'd let that stone crumble and discovered that I could still cry. I had to try not to break down in front of the family, I couldn't even begin to explain.

The pain of him not calling was getting unbearable. If a short time could affect me this much, what would I have been like if I'd become more involved.

* * * * *

A week later I was coming out of the newsagents down the road when I heard someone call out my name. I looked round and couldn't see anyone, so I continued walking.

'Pushpa,' someone shouted. I looked towards a white van that had pulled up alongside the curb and he was there, stepping out of the van.

I felt heat rise through my body. 'Hello,' I said – except it came out more as a squeak.

This was only the third time that I had actually seen him face to face; I preferred talking on the phone, as that was safer. I was conscious that I was wearing paint-splashed jeans and t-shirt as I had been decorating at home and was also worried somebody would see us and tell my father.

I walked towards the van and he smiled and started to explain..

Since he had come back home from London it had been really difficult to get to the phone without his family all listening in. Their family business did not close till late and his family was usually up till after midnight.

I felt huge relief that he had not simply lost interest as I feared. Whilst my logical mind told me that we had not known each other that long and there were no reason for him to continue to call me, my emotional side felt so strongly that logic went out of the window.

Jim asked if it was okay to call so late. I did want him to call me so suggested we agreed the specific days and times so I could be near the phone and not disturb my family.

We decided he would call on Friday. I made my way home much happier.

He called right on time on Friday night and he asked if we could meet up on Sunday.

'I can't go out in the evening. as that would be very unusual for me and my father will probably catch on that something is going on. We could meet up in the afternoon, though,' I explained.

'Great,' he said. 'I will see you near the church at the end of your road.'

Now I had to work out what to tell my father and the rest of the family. I felt really guilty and was determined not to lie; I never had and was not going to start now. My father trusted my every word and I had never betrayed that trust. Since my mum had gone I had always been there for him.

In the end, after much hesitation, I told them I was going out with a friend, whom of course they all thought they knew. I had always introduced my friends to my family, it is something, which I still do today. I don't know why it is important to have the approval of the people I am with, and especially my family. Having told them that I now prayed that they would not ask me any difficult questions.

After lunch on Sunday, I cleared up and started to get ready. Nothing out of the ordinary, as I did not want my family to be suspicious. Besides I did not have the greatest wardrobe and anyway this is who I was – no make-up, cropped hair and simple clothes. I think he must have liked the way I was or why would he ask to see me again?

As I walked towards the church I could see his metallic blue car parked there, my heart started pounding. I could see him watching me from the side mirror, which made me more nervous. Then I caught the smile in his eyes and felt better.

I got into the passenger seat.

'Are you all right?' he looked down at me.

'Yes,' I said, anxious in case any passersby recognised me.

'Where would you like to go?' he asked.

'I don't know,' I said, rather lamely. 'You choose.'

Jim started driving and wherever we were going it seemed to be a long way. I didn't mind, just being with him was enough, it didn't matter where we went. He surprised me and took me to the most beautiful man-made lake I had ever seen, in fact it was the only one I had seen. There were people on boats, water-skiing, picnicking on the grass. The sun was hot, it was beautiful and the water was blue and so clear.

We sat there for over three hours, talked, listened to music and admired the environment around us, it was magnificent. Sometimes we talked, sometimes we sat in compatible silence. It didn't matter.

This is how we would spend most of our Sundays from then on. When he was tired and put his seat back to sleep for a while, I loved to watch him. I became less nervous with him and even relaxed enough to sleep too, it was just so peaceful there.

He drove me back home to make sure I was in between 5 and 6 pm. The only other times I would see him were when he would turn up outside my workplace just to give me a lift home.

I knew that first Sunday (even though it was only our fourth meeting) that my feelings for him were more than just liking. I was worried that he was my first boyfriend, and wondered if what I was feeling was just normal. I was scared that I was vulnerable, after all this was my dream – someone who cared about me, who was fun and who I cared about. It was weird to know that I was thinking about somebody else apart from my extended family. I thought about him all the time, visualising our moments together, with every cell revolving around thoughts of him. If that was what love was, then, yes, I had already fallen in love with him.

We never really spoke about how we felt for each other until much later on. When the winter months came we still went to the lakes, but would leave early, as it was cold and the nights were drawing in earlier. Sometimes he would take me for a drink, but was always aware of the time and would ensure that he got me home safely so not to worry my father and brothers.

Fifteen months went by so quickly I could not believe it had been that long and the next thing I knew it was my eighteenth birthday coming up. To this day he had never ever attempted to touch me other than when he casually put his hand on my back, come to think about it nor had he introduced me to any of his friends, which I thought was really unusual, but relieved in case someone told my father.

It was two days before my eighteenth birthday that he sealed our relationship with our first kiss. It is very difficult to explain how I felt, it may seem ridiculous, but when I got home I looked in the mirror to see if my lips had changed in some way.

I also found out why he had not let me meet any of his friends, it was because of my age; he was 26 and I was 16 when we had first met. Those friends that he had told about me were already calling him a cradle snatcher.

Once during the Indian Dance festival I returned home and saw Jim outside my house, it was already 10.30pm. I had only started going to the festival when my sister moved back to Leicester so that we could accompany each other.

'Would you like to go dancing with me?' he asked naming a place where the dances were being held till late.

'Hang on, I'll ask my brothers,' I said in a moment of madness. I raced inside and my brothers said it was okay.

As we drove away I was sure my brother-in-law had seen us, as he'd come to check that I had got home safely after I dropped off my sister. I was so worried that I told him I could not take the risk of anyone seeing us again. I was still terrified that my father would find out. Our relationship was not in the tradition of our community and didn't reflect well on either of our families' reputations.

I still had a lot of things I wanted to do in life, but also I had promised myself that I would not leave my dad or brothers. I wanted to finish my education at some point before settling down to a married life. So, even though feeling for him the way I did and being aware and scared of what might have happened, I knew nothing could come of our relationship, but I chose to ignore that for now.

One Sunday just before Christmas I decided that it was getting far too serious for me. I was very aware of the strong feelings I had for him and decided that he needed to know how I felt. I was too much of a coward to tell him face to face so I decided to write my feelings down in a letter. The letter said everything about our relationship, my hopes and fears, how I felt about being with him and how I felt about my family. I gave him the letter to read and wanted to run away before he read it, but he insisted that I stay there until he had finished reading.

At first he laughed, and then realised I was serious. 'If you want to finish your education and look after your brothers, that is fine by me, but I don't see any reason why we cannot continue to meet,' he said.

I was scared of my feelings and tried to show him that the reason for wanting to call a halt was not how strong my feelings were becoming for him, but because I felt a responsibility and obligation to my family.

It did not blend in with the future that I had planned out and I was confused as to what decision to take. I knew I wanted more from him than a casual relationship, but also knew that it may not even end up as anything like that because I was scared of commitment and did not know the extent of his feelings or how far he wanted our relationship to go.

I told Jim I did not think that it was right for me to lie to my family and said I was too young to make a definite commitment. With my parents reputation to consider and I would do nothing that would tarnish that. Eventually, he gave in and accepted that I meant it.

So that was it. I yearned for him; I cried silently for weeks, the pain was unbearable at times, but I kept telling myself that I had been through worse whilst grieving for my mother over many years. Whilst I knew that it had been my choice to end things, I felt sorry for myself thinking that I had got all the bad luck and maybe was not entitled to the joys of a relationship yet.

Christmas came and went. After Christmas I was in my room and went to close the curtains, I looked out and there was his car outside the house. Then I saw him waving for me to come down. I felt such a relief to see him there, yet confused and afraid of how strong my feelings still were.

It was so natural for me to go to the passenger side and sit down, he started the car, and I panicked.

'No, I can't go with you!' I said in a rush.

He pulled up around the corner where he always had when he dropped me off from work and turned the engine off.

'I just thought we could still meet sometimes, if that is okay with you,' he started to say.

I stopped myself from shouting 'YES!' in his ear, and managed to say 'Let's take each day as it comes.'

He smiled. 'I will call you.' He paused. 'Would you like to go for a drink now?'

'No, I must get home; it's late,' I said.

We said our goodbyes and I got out and walked back round the corner and up the road to our house.

This was all wrong. How would my family my father react if he knew what was going on? I knew I had to stop it and remind myself of main objective in life was to look after my family and love them not to hurt them or tarnish our reputation.

The generations of girls that I belonged to were starting to adapt to Western life, and many were living a lifestyle totally different to what was expected of them. I was very old-fashioned, maybe I chose to be this way and I knew that was what was expected of me. I was torn between my obligation to the traditions of my culture and the expectations of my family and an urge to go out and see the outside world. No wonder I was confused!

FOUR

The Door I Chose To Open

I started making the decisions that would affect me, my 7 brothers that were still at home and my father, at a very young age. My brothers ranging from eight to twenty-two years in age, so I was almost a mother to the younger ones, and, although the older ones were older than me, I still looked after them.

Somehow I found that I had stopped making the decisions and was just being obliging doing whatever was required from me. Others had started making the decisions. Now I was at the beginning of another era, in a position to make the most powerful decisions of my life. After three years of being a nobody and living a low profiled meaningless existence, still grieving for my mum – life had changed and I could see a path ahead of me.

I have made life-changing decisions from the age of eleven. To let go of my childhood and take on adult responsibilities had affected my life to such an extent that I am still living with the decision today. By that I mean that I literally ignored what I really wanted and made no effort to make something of my life. Instead I did what I thought I ought to be doing, taking into account all the additional responsibilities that I had on board. My decisions were only made to benefit others and ensure that they did not hurt.

My first decision in life was deciding how I was going to carry on with my life without my mother. I decided to live in a virtual world imagining that she had not really left me, but was around and I would bump into her some day soon. I was living in an imaginary world.

I wanted my mum. I'd always believed that, if you set your mind on something and you really want it, it will come. But my mum never came back. When I could not cope with the loneliness or the pressure of other things I would talk to her and be angry with her for giving me birth and then leaving me to grow up on my own without her love and guidance.

I finished my education at secondary school and went on to college. My results were not that brilliant, but under the circumstances I was relieved simply to have passed all my exams. I hardly had time to study and felt tired all the time. I had no friends at college - there was no reason to. I had nothing in common with the others, they were still children and I was running a household. I was a loner, never mixed with anybody and kept everyone at arm's length in case they suggested that we do something together.

I was happy to be on my own in lessons and happy to sit at home all the other times, although I didn't do much sitting! I felt safe there and once all the cooking, shopping and cleaning had been done I could just relax or listen to music in my room. I danced in front of the mirror and imagined myself finding my dream husband and being a beautiful bride, just like in films.

The tight budget I had to run the household meant not being able to buy modern clothes like other girls my age wore. I sewed up my brother's old jeans so they looked more fashionable and wore their jumpers. After I lost my mum, I became one of the boys with short-cropped hair, jeans and a baggy top.

As I grew older and saw what was happening to others in third world countries and in the ghettos, where there were hundreds of orphans living in poverty on the streets I realised that I was really quite well off. I had my health, a roof over my head, my father and my brothers.

It was much later that I realised that I also had the ability to make life the way I wanted it. I only acknowledged this after another tragedy had hit me. I began to realise that I was so lucky to be in the position that I was. Not only was I being ungrateful, but also selfish by withholding all the good things I could give to the world besides money. I could give time and love.

Hence our meetings continued, we would still go to the lakes on Sundays and he would still pick me up from work whenever he could. I had no idea that my brother's wife who was related to him, had already approached his family for regarding my hand in marriage to him.

Eventually I discovered that they had seen me with him and, rather than approach me directly, they decided to sort it all out amongst themselves without telling me. I have no idea why they decided not to talk to me and ask me if this was what I wanted. The first I knew about it was when my eldest brother told me what had happened and said that they were waiting for his family to get back to us. I told him there and then that I don't want to marry yet, I still have my goals, my brothers, and my father, and how could I contemplate on leaving them just yet.

I was very angry with my elder brother Mo for interfering and that, although I loved Jim very dearly, I knew I was not yet ready for marriage.

When I spoke to him next, Jim told me what had happened and how his family had approached him with the same suggestion.

He had also said 'no' to the marriage yet, but was under a lot of pressure because of his age. He made sure that he did not mention to his family that we were seeing each other, as they may not have agreed with that and, of course, it would not have been good for my reputation.

His family were pushing to him to say yes, they were also aware that I wanted to continue my studies and suggested that I could continue them after the marriage took place. They wanted the wedding that year.

I was confused. Things were moving really fast and I didn't seem to have much say in things. My brothers and sisters were split in how they felt about him and his family.

His family were concerned about his age. They were a very strict and dominant Asian family that expected a lot of hard work from whoever was going to marry their son.

His parents met my brothers to discuss the dowry. During that discussion they stated that I had to be very strong as they wanted commitment, there was a lot of lifting to do, long hours and I would be expected to do a lot of work in their business. This was enough to freak my brothers out, but they assured his family that I was really hard working.

I knew I was really strong, I had come this far under very difficult circumstances, carried home very heavy bags of shopping every week, done all the cleaning and gone to work. What could they throw at me that could be any more difficult?

I spoke to him again and told him my concerns. He reassured me that everything would be okay and that we should let the elders do what they thought was right and to let them do it according to tradition.

I agreed, but still didn't feel happy with the decision. His family wanted the wedding as soon as possible, but I wasn't ready for marriage yet. I was only eighteen, I wanted a career, and I wanted to continue to look after my father and my brothers for a while yet.

I asked my brothers what to do and they told me to go ahead as they would be fine, promised me that they would look after each other and themselves. My concern was my father, who would look after him? My younger brothers tried to reassure me that they would look after my father like we had all these years, and my elder brothers told me they would look after the whole family.

My in-laws-to-be were anxious to have the wedding as soon as possible. They had other plans for later that year and wanted to know the marriage had taken place first.

So that was it, before I knew it I had agreed to the date, the engagement and the civil ceremony at the registrar were to take place on12th May 1984. This was the official legal date of our wedding, but we would be not be living together until after the Asian traditional ceremony which would be held on 21st July 1984. This was the day I would move to my in-laws home and leave my family.

I remember thinking at the time that at least my father would feel that he had fulfilled the promise he had made to mum of seeing my hand given in marriage. As my husband-to-be was of the same caste as my family we would avoid all the issues that marrying out of caste created.

I felt suffocated for a time as there was so much to do, not only for the wedding but also to prepare my brothers to take over the household chores, cooking, paying bills and running the household.

I started teaching them how to cook. I also wrote all the recipes I knew in a book so that they knew exactly what to cook and how. I showed them the bills that would need paying and where I kept the jar of the housekeeping money. I had opened a bank account for the two younger brothers. I sorted out my mother's jewellery for their wives and a hundred other small tasks.

I told my father what needed to be done and begged him not to drink when I was married so that he could look after my brothers and not to burden them unnecessarily. He promised me he would.

As the days drew nearer, although the whole thing excited me I was still reluctant to leave my family. People everywhere assured me that this was the best thing I could do, they kept telling me it was okay and that this was good. At least I would be settled and could start living my own life and I would be happy - so everybody told me.

There was no doubt about that I was marrying somebody that I loved very much. I adored his very being, how mature and confident he was, his good looks, of which he was also aware, his assurance that he would look after me all my life, but most of all I loved his laughter and smile. I also loved him with every cell in my body, had faith in him and believed in his every word. I felt very proud to be able to walk next to him and loved it when people acknowledged his looks, his fit body and his engaging personality.

Throughout all the arrangements, instead of excitement about my wedding, I could not shake a continuous worry about leaving my family behind. I tried to think positively and hoped for the best. The days were drawing close, I was feeling suffocated.

On the engagement day everything was magic, I felt in every step that I took, the bride-to-be and felt very proud to be standing next to him. It was overwhelming, my brothers had done an amazing job in arranging everything and making the day happen. His family wanted a big event as he was the last child in their family of seven children to get married. The costs were more than we had anticipated but we managed somehow.

This was the end of my adolescence and, although it was not that eventful, those years were magical to me. I still laugh today at the great times I had during this period in my life. I hardly recall any of the memories of the bad times, such as how we got through when we had minimum resources, when it was daunting to be at home on my own. The times I had with my family were some of the happiest and fun years of my life. We managed to balance being children with the maturity we needed to cope without our mother. We made the years the best we could under the circumstances and made the most of what we did have.

In addition to that my husband gave me a taste of what life was like outside my family environment. I learned what it was like do new things and to be with somebody special. He gave me the magic when I had lost hope of ever finding love and I believed from the depths of my soul that our meeting was inevitable.

Even though he was much older than me I think because I had to grow up really quickly I would have been uncomfortable with somebody younger. Jim would look after me and provide me with all the love and care I desperately craved from life. He was my inspiration and my light; I would have done anything for him.

I chose to be very traditional and respectful through out my married life and lived life as was expected of me as a married woman in an Asian household. I was always conscious that I needed to be a good and obliging daughter-in-law, as I suspect the case may still be today in many Asian households.

Most of the women I knew that had come from India, especially my hubby's mates wives were more modern and westernised than I was. They asked me why I continued to wear a sari everyday. I told them that I wanted to be traditional and did it out of respect for my husband's family.

More surprising was when I went to India with hubby, my daughter and my father-in-law. Again I found the women there to be more westernised than myself. I really was an old-fashioned girl.

I suppose you could say that I gained a set of parents when I married my husband, but there was a huge difference between your own parents and your in-laws. With your own parents you don't have to prove yourself every day and you certainly don't rate second best in comparison to the other children. When I used to see my in-laws with their children I wished that I could be treated the same way as they were. I wanted that affection and easy connection, but there was always a differential between the daughters and daughter in-law.

My decision to get married could have been viewed in many different ways now that I think about it. It was difficult and sad because I was leaving my freedom, my dearest family to be with a highly reputable and dominant family. I knew that they expected a lot and only perfection would do. I would not have freedom of choice.

At least my father would live in peace knowing that he had fulfilled the last thing my mother had asked of him and thinking that his daughter was settled in a very happy environment. I had married somebody in the caste and, because of this, my parents respect and reputation remained intact. I felt that, at least, I did my parents justice and abided by what was then required by a girl in an Asian tradition.

So dreams can come true if you really truly believe in them, but to gain a life of fulfillment with my soul mate I sacrificed my life with my brothers and my father. I know that when I met my husband and started to panic because of the love I was growing for him, it was because I was really afraid of losing him as I did my mother. Of course, I had convinced myself that I was not worthy of any attention from anybody, so, at first, it was hard for me to accept that someone cared that much for me. For me to move on in life I knew I would have to change my attitude and accept that it was my time to have all that I had desired as a little girl. It was simply a matter of how I would fare as a married woman.

FIVE

The Door Is Open

People feel fearful for many reasons; it could be when they are making the smallest decision or a big life-impacting decision, or meeting people, or applying for jobs. How people deal with their fear depends on their personality and life experiences. Some people may never deal with their fears and continue to live life in fear forever.

Fear became a part of me after my mother died. During the days that followed her passing it dawned on me just how lonely and empty my life was going to be. I saw my life stretching ahead of me and knew that it was going to be a very frightening journey. I had not yet developed confidence. I'd never had to make the effort to make friends; at primary school the girls approached me to become their friend. I had made friends in the same way at secondary school before my mother passed on. If they had not come to me I could have spent the entire five years on my own.

These friends were companions at school, but we did not do anything together outside school, as I did not have the time for them. Every time they asked me if I wanted to get involved, panic bells would ring inside me, warning me of how I should be as a traditional Asian girl. Their world was alien to me; I had responsibilities to look after the household, particularly my father when he was having one of his drinking bouts. Friendships outside of school were definitely not for me.

I knew I had to do something about this or my entire life would go by without me ever really having any friends or somebody I could call my soul friend. Despite knowing this I was afraid to make contact with other people. Whatever I did from now on it would be for the benefit of my family and it did not really matter what I was missing out on. I was afraid that if I did make contact with others they would demand my time and I did not have time to spare. I did not even have time to study, let alone to be sociable.

Gradually I became more of a recluse and I would make any excuse to get out of situations that required me to talk to people I didn't know. I was happy to sit at home do the housework and watch television with my brothers, my father and our pets. I did not realise then that this was the road I would take for most of my life. What was going on outside my world did not bother me, what I did not know, I did not miss.

There were times I used to wonder what it would be like to be one of the girls living a normal life in a western society. I wondered what it would be like to be able to go to each others houses, cinemas and have the money just to go into town to do some girly shopping, I would snap myself out of daydreams telling myself that I did not deserve all this.

Looking back I would have been better off to make friends, at least that little bit of friendship and companionship would have given me some distraction from the isolated life I was living at the time. But, I adored my family; spending time with my brothers and my father was a joy to me. I felt privileged to look after them, to know how to run a household successfully; I really did enjoy what I did.

All this helped me to become the mature person I was. I became such a good cook that I was cooking for hundreds of people at one time at family gatherings – our own and, then I was asked to help with friends' parties too. This gave me some kudos with my new in-laws and my husband, as they were excellent cooks and had very discerning tastes where food was concerned.

Many people have some regrets from their childhood; if I admit to the truth, I regret missing those years between childhoods and being an adult. I was catapulted from childhood into the maturity needed to manage a household full of people, all relying on me.

Sometimes I would blame God for putting me on this earth;. for everything that I did not have and for taking my mum from me at such a young age. Then I would get angry with myself for being so selfish and not appreciating what we already had. My brothers had suffered the same loss, she was their mother too. Some people in the world did not even have a roof over their heads, or had lost both parents and did not have any siblings. How lucky I was; I had my brothers, my sisters and my father.

I was told that I could study to complete my education once I was married. My elder brothers and sister had assured me that they would look after my father and the brothers I was leaving behind. But even as I agreed to take the advice of my family and marry at the age of just eighteen, I knew deep down that completing my education was not going to happen. My husband had mentioned several times about extending the family business. He would need my help and had already asked if I would mind helping him.

I would have done anything for him, as he was aware. So, I committed to ensuring that his business would be successful with my help.

* * * * *

The wedding came and I had a very heavy heart. I missed my mother terribly, especially during the days leading up to it. I still felt confused about what I was doing, guilty for leaving my family, feeling the loss and support of my mother and feeling really selfish about why I was doing it. I didn't feel as though I deserved happiness and love.

My wedding should be the happiest day of my life and, in many ways, it was a happy day. But inside a part of me was so sad. I was happy that I had ensured that my father had fulfilled his promise to my mother.. I was proud of him too; he had stopped drinking several weeks before the wedding and was sober throughout the preparations, ceremonies and the actual day.

It was happy and sad – and a really tiring day. The emotion of leaving my family overcame me and I cried a lot with my brothers and sisters at the end of the day. I felt a mess when I reached my in-laws.

As we approached the house my husband's five sisters were blocking the doorway. It was tradition not to let the bride and groom into the house until they agreed to give something valuable, or whatever was asked for, to their sisters. I waited patiently while my husband agreed on what he was going to give.

We each put five dots of the red powder on the doorframe to acknowledge our new sacred home together. Finally, we were allowed to walk through the door. Our families were both well respected and there had been over a thousand people at the wedding. I was so glad to be able to sink into a hot bath and relax after that day.

I was very aware of my new environment. My new family appeared to be more superior to my own family. I rapidly realised that I was going to have to learn, and learn fast, to survive with these people. I could not even speak Gujarati properly, although I understood it fluently, this was because nobody at home had spoken it; even my father only used a few basic words mostly speaking English.

A few days after the wedding my father-in-law commented on how quiet I was. He had not realised the limitations of my language skills. This was especially challenging as my new family spoke in a classical version of Gujarati, which was even more difficult to learn.

This was the first day of the rest of my life. I was living with a family that I had never spoken to or even exchanged a few words with. At eighteen that was daunting. Although I had matured through my experiences I felt very young and vulnerable in front of them. I was afraid of appearing naive and stupid, because my background was simple compared to theirs.

I decided that, until they told me otherwise, I would stick to the traditions to ensure I showed them respect. I wore a sari and covered my head in the early days. I would not go into room if my father and brother-in-law were in the room. Eventually, my mother-in-law told me that there was no need for me to cover my head, but I continued to wear a sari every day no matter what I was doing.

I did enjoy wearing them and Jim loved them. He thought if they were worn with the right top and jewellery, they looked very attractive and, of course, a sari can be very sexy. He loved blue, green and red ones, and told me how much he liked me in a really nice sari with all the accessories – matching bangles, bindis and gold jewellery or silver. He didn't like artificial jewellery and felt proud when people used to tell him how good I looked. I felt really good too knowing how proud he was of me.

Jim went back to working in the shop straight away and I started work a week later. Apparently they had not booked a honeymoon, as his family had not yet decided whether we should go or not.

Three weeks later, my husband insisted that we should go; his sisters were right behind us. I felt really guilty because it would be their money that would be paying for the trip. The only money I had was a few hundred pounds that I had saved up over the years. I had some of my mother's jewellery, as I had only had the earrings I had worn at my sisters wedding. I had worn my mother's bangles at my wedding, but I promised myself I would have some made for me one day and fulfill my mother's wish. .

My in-laws asked for the dowry gifts that we were to give my husband according to tradition when the wedding arrangements were discussed. The bride's family traditionally paid for everything – the venue, the food, and all the other costs of the wedding day. Luckily my mum had had a gold 22-carat watchstrap already made for her future son-in-laws, even for me, although I was only six at the time they were made. The traditional Indian dowry was so important.

My family was still responsible for paying for the bridegroom's suit and other clothing and the ring. We scraped the money together from my housekeeping and my brothers contributed some. I wanted to leave as much as I could at home so my brothers and father would not be struggling to survive. It was some consolation that my older brothers were watching over them.

By this time I had realised that my husband did not have much say in what went on at home. He was mature and appeared to be very much in control in the outside world; at home everything was discussed with his parents and permission sought before we did anything. Whilst this was traditional in most Asian families, in Jim's family there was no flexibility, they stuck rigidly to the traditional way of doing things.

My family respected the traditions, but did not expect anybody to do anything unless they really wanted to. Had my mother been around things may have been different. She would have ensured that I still had long hair, that we all spoke and understood our language and origins perfectly. But, if my mum had been around, I would not have married at such an early age and I would have had an education.

I could sense there was also a friction between Jim and his only elder brother Bal. I discovered that they had had a very bad argument days before the wedding and were not talking. His brother was fine with me, although it took me several months to pluck up the courage to speak to Bal unless he spoke to me first. My husband's family consisted of his mum, dad, one elder brother and five sisters. As the younger brother, I think he always felt second best to his brother. His brother was a very proud man, like the whole family.

They were probably one of the richest families in the caste and they knew their status in the community, They were all tall people, my mother in- law being at least 5 ft 6, which is tall for Asian women, and my husbands brother well over six feet. At just five foot tall I felt tiny beside them.

My father-in-law had worked very hard all his life and because of him they had a successful business, a secure home and a comfortable living. Jim's job of extending the business by opening a new shop was on the horizon, although it seemed to have been delayed by the wedding.

Jim took time off from the business and we went into town to book the honeymoon. I was very excited. We searched for the best deal and found a week in Majorca, so we booked it. I could not wait, to be able to spend some time alone away from England with my husband. It was like a part of my dream coming true. Another reason for my excitement was that this would be my first trip on an airplane.

Everybody at work kept asking when we were going, so now I had a date.

We were due to leave at 10.00pm on Friday 29th August. It was now four weeks since the wedding and since I had seen my brothers and my father, so I asked Jim if we could visit them before we went on holiday. Even for this I had to ask permission, although my father's home was just a few miles away.

Permission was given and, on the day before we flew out, we went home. Only three brothers were at home and my father was asleep. I should have phoned first, but was afraid of asking to use the phone at my in-laws. I don't know what it was, but I felt guilty for using anything in their house. There was an atmosphere that made me feel uncomfortable. I put it down to being new to all this and unsure of what was expected or normal. I thought that, once I got used to them, things would settle down and they would be easier for me to approach.

So I arrived unannounced at my father's house.

'How are you all doing?' I asked Chandan.

He looked sad, but said, 'We're okay.' In my heart I knew they were missing me as much as I was missing them.

Jim said, 'You must come and visit us any time you like, Pushpa misses you, I know.' I knew they wouldn't come, because they would never feel comfortable there. But my brother nodded and said 'yes' and 'thank you' as was expected.

My father was sleeping, so I did not disturb him. My husband was disappointed, as he had wanted to talk to my father. Until now they had never sat down together for a talk.

Quietly, I asked my brother how my father was doing regarding his drinking and was relieved when my brother assured me that he had not touched a drop since the wedding. I hoped that he might stop drinking altogether now the pressure to see me settled was now gone. I told him I would try to come back the next day, because I really wanted to see Dad before we went on holiday.

Just after my marriage some of my brothers had told me how much they were missing me and even told me that even though they had experienced the loss of our mother, the loss of me felt even greater.

I missed them; I missed being my playful, free self instead of trying to be this ideal person that my in-laws expected me to be. At home I could be whom I wanted, a child or an adult. At my in-laws I did everything by the book because I didn't want my in-laws to think I had not been brought up properly; that would show a lack of respect for my parents. I wanted my in-laws' approval; I wanted them to say how good a daughter-in-law I was, and how proud they were to have me in their family.

My heart sank as I left my father's house. I felt sad and guilty. I loved my husband dearly, but wished that there was some way I did not have to leave my family like this. I felt like it was my wedding day all over again. I felt really emotional and only perked up at the thought that I could come back tomorrow and see Dad – and, if I was lucky, my other brothers. I hadn't asked my husband yet but would do later on.

I just could not for the life of me get my father out of my head; I knew I had to see him before we went. I cried silently inside on the journey home. What had I done? Why did I not wait another few years at least until my two younger brothers had left school? From the look of the house I knew none of my older brothers had been there to look after things as they had promised. I knew that I had not really had a choice, it had all happened in spite of me, but I still felt as though I should have been stronger and resisted.

What could I do? I could leave my husband and his family and come back home, it was still not too late, and there was always time for me to get settled later on in life. My marriage in these first few weeks was not as I had dreamed, but every day I hoped it would change.

Jim's family really was very autocratic and thought nothing of putting people down or making fun out of them. At first I thought it was a one-off but later came to realise that this was their nature.

My husband was always busy working; the only time we really had alone was at night. It didn't seem to bother him much, but then when he told me that he had spent the day thinking of me, as I did of him it made things all right.

That night I packed our clothes for the next day. I went to bed, but I was restless. I had to wake up early; here everybody woke up early and, as there was only one bathroom, you had to be quick! This day my mother-in-law decided she wanted to make poppadums. This was a hard process as the dough had to be kneaded a lot and many other processes had to take place. At 8am I was in the kitchen helping when the phone rang. It was for me.

I thought 'That's funny, who would be calling me here?' Nobody had ever called me in the four weeks that I had been here. I felt low inside as I picked up the receiver.

It was my eldest brother, Mo. 'Are you okay?' he asked.

'Yes,' I felt a bit annoyed, because I knew he had not been to visit my father or my brothers. I did not say anything as I was acutely conscious of my in-laws sitting behind me.

'Dad passed away this morning.'

The phone slipped from my hand. Everything went blank for a moment, then I managed to pick it up again. 'What happened?' I asked numbly.

'I don't know, Chandan found him,' he told me.

'I am on the way.' I said.

I felt dazed and confused. How could that be? How could this have happened?

I wanted to see him now; I had to speak to him, to tell him I was okay and not to worry. I wanted to apologise for all the times I had been angry with him. I wanted to tell him how sorry I was for having had to lock him in his room for his own safety when he had had far too much to drink. I wanted to tell him that I wish I had never left him. My head was buzzing – there was so much I wanted to say to him, but he was gone.

I walked into the kitchen and went to tell my mother-in-law, as she was the only one around, I think my husband had sneaked out to have a cigarette, I desperately needed to be held at this moment. The guilt I felt cancelled out any joy I had felt after my wedding. It seemed that the joys of life were not to be my destiny.

I did not even know what to say to my mother-in-law. What were the correct words, what was the word for death in our language? I remember blurting something out and then a few tears fell down my face. I wanted to be home with my family and have things back as they used to be. Suddenly I felt tired and weary, the early morning and late nights caught up with me.

I was still working at my old place and with Jim's family having a business that did not close till 10 pm we never managed to go to sleep before 12 pm. I was usually the first one up, as I had to leave to catch an early bus. The week after the wedding there was a month of fasting, which I did. I had never fasted in my life before, other than the odd Saturday when my mum was around. This time I had done the whole month, because everyone else in the household did it (except Jim who only managed one week) and it was expected. Fasting meant eating just one meal a day, but we could eat fruit and drink as much water or tea as we wanted all day. I had lost a lot of weight because of this and now I felt tired and weak.

My mother-in-law told me to change from my black sari to a white sari and went to find Jim to take me. I felt dazed and still numb, what was I doing here? Nothing else mattered, I just needed to be home. Guilt told me I should never have left.

I was hardly aware of the journey to my father's house. I could not think of it any other way – it would always be his house. When I arrived I ran through the door. All my brothers that had been with me all these years were there, and I hugged them very tightly. I felt guilt, remorse at leaving them and told them over and over again how sorry I was that I had left them.

I watched as the paramedics took my dad from the house. I was standing at the bottom of the stairs numb. I did not want him to leave like this; I wanted to see him walking down the stair, dressed up in his unique proud way. I never would see him like that again.

The inevitable twelve mourning days passed. When my mother had died we were young and unaware of much of what went on, this time we were older and took more notice. People came, people brought food, everyone sang religious songs and then there was the funeral.

My dad looked extremely thin. I learned from my brothers that he had really cut back on his food a lot. They told me that he had said that there was nobody to look after him now, and also that he had felt a sense of relief that I was now married. He had fulfilled his promise to my mother and felt at peace now and could do anything he wanted.

He had died of a heart attack in his sleep. My youngest brother had gone to him in the morning and found him. That was reassuring; at least he had not been in pain or suffered long as my mother had. I knew that a lot of people, including my in-laws had talked badly of my father and his drinking, so I was relieved that I could tell them that his death was not drink-related. I know he had experienced much heartache since the loss of my mother, as we had never experienced that sort of loss, the loss of your spouse, we could not possibly understand how he felt. Perhaps he had, literally, died of a broken heart.

I know how much loss I felt since my mum had gone; I could not even imagine what he must have gone through with seven sons and one daughter still studying, a single parent and little income. It was enough to make anybody panic. Whilst I know it was wrong to turn to drink, but the only way he could cope with it all emotionally when it got really bad was to have a drink and not stop for a few weeks. I don't think he had any idea how difficult it was for us to watch him destroying himself. I knew that he had not drunk since I left and I held onto that and felt very proud of him.

During the mourning period I just kept going over and over what had made me decide to get married so quickly. I had no answer to the question of why I left my family who needed me? I began to think that maybe I could come back here and look after my brothers. I did not know my way into the future.

People kept commenting on how gaunt and weary I looked. I dismissed it, but I was really tired and on the day I came home I slept downstairs in front of my parents picture for hours. I could vaguely hear people coming and going, but nothing could rouse me.

My relatives noticed a bruise on my arm. It had been an accident when my husband was playing around. I don't think they believed me when I told them it was an accident.

The honeymoon had to be cancelled and was never discussed again. I would never forget the date that my father passed away; it was the 29th of August, the day before my birthday. What a day to remember, to feel the guilt forever for leaving him. I could not help thinking again and again that, if I had stayed, he would still be around today.

When the time came for me to go back to my in-laws home after the 14th day, I felt lonely, confused and could not stop my crying. My brothers assured me that they would look after the remaining brothers and not let anything happen to them, but they hadn't done before and I left with a very heavy heart.

I felt as if my life was over even before it had begun. I knew I would not be able to contact my brothers, because it was just so awkward at my in laws to do anything. I told them I would come back really soon and made them promise me that they would look after each other.

I left, thinking that it should have been me sorting things out at my father house, not them. I was worrying about how they would cope.

SIX

The Heaviest Door

Following my fathers passing, I returned to my new life now in very different circumstances. The next few months went in a blur. I continued to go to work which helped enormously emotionally for me as at least I could be my self there. I felt suffocated at home and felt I could not grieve my family and my father because we were always so busy. I also think that as my in-laws had not experienced the loss of a loved one for a very long time they had no idea of what I was going through.

Jim was really sympathetic, but I don't think he realised just how low I was feeling. The rest of his family expected me to carry on as normal. I desperately needed to be comforted by his parents, but there would always be a barrier. I wasn't their daughter and, although I know that they did care for me very deeply, it was not the same. They didn't show their feelings in that way and, in any case, I was not their daughter, only a daughter-in-law. In my family it had been different; we would hug and tell each other 'I love you'. However, my mother-in-law was very close to her daughters and you could see the admiration and love a mile off. That was what I really missed.

In many Asian families the parents want their children to marry and settle. However, even though the marriage is arranged and the parents have chosen the spouse, they are not treated as part of the family and always remain an 'outsider'.

On catching up with my brothers, a month later, I found that they had decided to sell the house and the younger brothers would go to live in the homes of their three elder brothers. It would save the costs of running an extra home. I let them get on with it. I felt that I no longer had a say in the matter, because I now belonged to Jim and his family.

I was really hurt that they had decided to sell the house and knew for a fact that had I still been at home I would never have sold it. Although they decided to split the money from the sale between the twelve of us, I told them that I did not want a share. That money should go to my younger brothers to be invested in their future.

It would have been nice if they had asked me my opinion; but they didn't. They didn't even ask if I would like to keep some of the things that we had accumulated over the years. To this day I still do not know where everything went: my mum's massive cooking pots, my dads clothing, ornaments, my hi-fi system and the vinyl record collection that we had built up. Everything disappeared.

In the end, all my brothers and sisters kept their share. Jim agreed with me, so I split my share into three, one third each to go to my two youngest brothers and the third share went to a child that I sponsored in Africa.

I wondered if I would ever get over the enormous guilt I felt for leaving my dad and my brothers. I was now tied to a family with no escape and with very little contact with my family. My crying continued, for the loss of my mum, my decision to marry, the loss of my father and my brothers losing their beloved home that my parents had worked so hard to keep running.

If I did ever want to visit my family where would I go? Whose home would be the main point of contact? There was already friction between my elder brothers over trivial things and I felt that my family was fragmented.

* * * * *

Life at my new home continued the same as usual. I got up early, bathed and went to work. My father-in-law opened the business; my mother-in-law got on with all the cooking and shopping during the day and Jim and his brother would go to the cash and carry or serve customers in the business. Jim's sister-in-law washed the clothes, did the cleaning and then, later in the day, would help out in the shop.

At work I was away from all this and I could laugh, communicate with people and feel free. At home I talked only to Jim late at night, after the business closed and everybody had had dinner and settled for the night. Because I could not yet speak Gujarati properly I was reluctant to speak to anybody. I didn't even talk much to Jim in front of the family, as he would tease me, as did his family.

On my return from work I changed from my work clothes to a sari every day and then, either helped my mother-in-law in the kitchen or helped in the shop. I could never just go and sit and put my feet up as my husband and his family did. When there was nothing else to do I would go to our room and sit there till they came up from closing the business for the day. This was usually after 10.30pm – and then we would have dinner.

By the time everyone had eaten and discussed the events of the day, and we had cleared up it was after midnight. It started to take its toll on me; I felt tired at work all the time and would sometimes fall asleep. I travelled to and from work by bus, Jim would sometimes meet me at lunchtime and I really looked forward to this, it was our special 'alone' time.

The honeymoon was never mentioned again. After our wedding day we did not even spend a few days on our own. I was disappointed, but didn't pursue the matter. Maybe it was not meant to be, maybe I didn't deserve one, especially after making the decision to marry and leave all my family behind. Months later I was still riddled with guilt for what had happened with my dad. Even though I knew that he had fulfilled my promise to my mother I was still suffering from remorse.

Jim occasionally mentioned that he wanted to go on holiday, just the two of us. He said, 'Let's go on a proper honeymoon' at intervals throughout our marriage and I could not understand why he did not just go and book one. But I was never brave enough to challenge him and I really felt that it was not my place to say anything, so it never happened.

The times I spent with my husband on our own were fantastic, but never enough. It was not that I resented being with the family; I loved having a family around me. I grew to love his family very dearly. I had nothing but respect for my hubby's brother, which would make Jim angry sometimes. I discovered that, although there was a lot of love and respect between the two brothers, Jim resented the fact that his parents listened more to his elder brother and didn't always take notice of him.

Jim tended to do things his own way, as and when he liked. Out of respect I did things the way his parents wanted, because I wanted them to feel proud of me. It was important that they knew that, despite not having a mother, I was still a well-brought up girl. I encouraged Jim to do the same. Sometimes he would, but often he resented being told what to do – whether I was telling him or his parents were.

Sometimes he complained that I did things their way, but I always felt that it was important to respect their decisions. I knew that they would never tell me to do anything that would do me any harm. Throughout our lives together I always listened to them more often then he liked, which sometimes caused upset between us. I often told him that life is too short and we did not know how long we had each other. I encouraged him to make the most of it while we could, to make each moment count. At the time I had no idea how short that time might be.

I had experienced the death of my own parents. I was left to carry on with my life wishing that things had been different, wishing that we had said things differently, but it was too late. Jim listened to me whilst I grieved, but not for long. He had never experienced hardship or lost somebody he loved beyond life itself. He was always laughing and happy; I could not imagine him being sad or crying. Angry? Yes, he had a very short temper. He moved through life living for today and never thought about the future much at all.

* * * * *

Before I knew it, Christmas was upon us, my first Christmas with my new family. I drifted back to our celebrations last Christmas. We had had a great time, all my brothers who lived at home, my father and me. We had sung carols, given presents, did pile ups, fought for chocolates and watched television. I missed that environment so much and Christmas without them was going to be hard.

This year Jim's sisters and their families would come for a few days. This meant that I would be helping my mother-in-law in the kitchen, serving and being ready to run to get things, in case anybody wanted something.

The shop stayed open until 2 pm, so dinner was served after this, along with a few drinks. This was the way most festive days were celebrated at this house. Half a day on Christmas day was the only day that we closed throughout the whole year.

I had been pregnant with my daughter at the age of nineteen. We were ecstatic, but I knew that the pressure was on my husband to open a second shop.

During my pregnancy I carried on working in my job, while my husband prepared the business, and I would go to help him after work. After Kajal was born, Jim suggested I give up my job to help him in the business.

I was very excited about starting up our own shop, but realised that I was giving up the little independence and freedom I had. Once I had taken this step I knew there would be no going back; I would never have the courage to ask if I could go out to work again. I wanted my husband to be successful, so I put that behind me to look forward to the challenge and, of course, to being together for most of the day in our own environment.

There was a flat above the shop and Jim started to sleep there to ensure that the shop was secure and safe from burglary. At first I stayed at my in-laws, but, as the business grew, I moved in with Kajal a few months later. Even then we still had to go for our meals at the main house. I felt guilty for leaving my mother-in-law to prepare the meals, so I went to help her out as early as I could. This meant a lot of the work for the shop, such as stock lists, cashing up and the general paperwork had to be done in the early hours of the morning when we got back.

Our business started to grow rapidly and soon we asked if we could move to the flat properly and run our own household. We were only down the road so it was not that bad and we would still be one family.

My in-laws provided us with all the furniture from their previous home and my mother-in-law gave me the utensils for the kitchen. I settled down to making my own home – trying not to think of the last time I had run a household.

Even though we now lived in our own place I was still acutely conscious of the need to continue living to their standards. This meant keeping the business and our home in immaculate condition, growing the business and still ensuring that we did everything right – only after seeking guidance from the family. As they were business people, their attitude was that money should be spent sparingly and that is exactly how we did spend it. If I wanted something I would ask Jim, in turn, he would ask his family. We did not really have to go shopping much, because we had everything we needed in the business and my in-laws bought Asian groceries for us in the early years.

My negotiation skills grew; I excelled at buying stock and also was a very good sales person. We were praised by everybody for how great the premises looked. Even the health inspectors said 'If everybody had their businesses in this condition we would definitely be out of business!'

However, it was a trying time. We worked long hours, seven days a week. Kajal lived behind the counter as we got busier. Luckily the kitchen was behind us, so I could prepare her food quite easily. I had to cook really early in the morning so that no food smells lingered in the shop while it was open. By 7.00 am I would have cooked the evening meal and prepared any other food we needed for the day, so I would have little to do, apart from serving up, later.

Like my in-laws business we never closed until 10.30pm – and still ate really late. However, unlike before, I never used to feel tired and just carried on. Jim had a nap in the afternoons, as they all did at his home. I don't know where my energy came from, but I didn't seem to need that rest, which was just as well as I really didn't have time!

The customers used to love us and started to call us Mr. and Mrs. 'Cheap', as we used to have good bargains. Some people from those days still call me that! Jim was amazing with everybody. He had charisma and attracted a phenomenal amount of custom with his cheeky laughter and the way he chatted to people. I loved watching him in action. As I'd married him at eighteen you could say that I almost grew up with his family, so I learnt a lot from them. But from Jim I learned not only how to become successful in business, but how to enjoy it too.

As my children were both with me in the business all day and there was a constant flow of customers, it was impossible for me to do anything for a long period of time such as playing games or reading a book. So I taught them how to read, write and identify colours with products in the business. The labels were short and easy to remember, it also helped me when I needed things from the store they were able to fetch it for me.

Both kids were able to read and write by the time they were two or three years old; hence they were ahead of most children when they started school. I was also fortunate to get them into the best school available (apart from a private one); it was a Roman Catholic school and about two miles from our home. They only accepted ten percent of non-Catholic students and they had to wear uniforms. I was really proud of the kids. Jim agreed with me that it was a good idea for them to go to this school rather than a local school. Better still, a bus stopped right outside the shop, which made taking them to school really easy.

By this time I had become, according to a lot of people, an excellent cook! My father-in-law, who was an excellent chef and taught me to cook everything that my husband loved. One of Jim's sisters taught me lots of both savoury and sweet recipes. Although I helped my mother-in-law in the kitchen it was basically assisting her and doing things that would help her with cooking the main dishes. She was also a brilliant cook and had cooked for hundreds of people at a time.

Through her I learnt to do the same as did my husband. We would cook for parties, occasions, gatherings, and sports events and have people over. It was very hard to say no to others when they asked me to do something, and I realised that it was tiring me out. The main reason for this was because the kitchen was next to the business, I could not cook while we were open, so sometimes I would be up all night cooking and preparing.

I did not mind doing it for my husband or the family, I used to love watching him enjoy his food as much as he did so when he used to go and buy the ingredients for me to cook with. My children really enjoy their freshly cooked food because of this and have developed the same tastes as their father. I gradually started to say no to people, because not only was I doing all the cooking in my time, but also always ended up using my ingredients. I knew some of them resented this, me refusing, but I used to explain why and used to feel really hurt when they did not accept the reason and gradually contact with them was reduced.

I always felt I had to make excuses for so many things in my life because I just could not refuse people any thing they asked of me and the main reason was that I was afraid of rejection, I just wanted to be accepted by everyone, I felt so guilty after saying no, that sometimes I would call back and tell them I had changed my mind and make an excuse for the initial excuse.

The years went by quite quickly and before we knew it 13 Christmases had past. After the last one we decided to lease the shop out. My husband wanted to spend more time living a normal life and doing things such as going shopping or going on holidays as a family, do things we were not allowed to do so freely because of the restrictions of the business. I also welcomed the idea. We had, since our marriage, been on five holidays as a family in nineteen years. These were a week in the Isle of Wight when I was eight months pregnant with my daughter, a week down to Cornwall when my daughter was four years old, about four weeks in India with my father-in-law when my daughter was seven, four weeks in America when she was 10 and my son 5 and finally a fortnight in Turkey a couple of years later.

In addition to this Jim had been on his own to India and Africa twice. He had many mini breaks as well with his friends whilst I ran the business. However, this time my husband did have a dream. He wanted us to go on holiday to Africa as a family, also he still did not give up on the idea that we would still be going on our honeymoon. However, later on in life, in the last few years he was quite persistent that he wanted to have a holiday with just the two of us as we had never had the opportunity to do so.

Unfortunately the holiday never happened. What led to it never happening was the fact that he became ill after his trip to India, which was a year and half after we had leased the business as I mentioned before. He was ill over a couple of years. During the last year he had been hospitalised 3 times and the last time he went in he did not want anyone to know. I made that decision to respect his wishes; I was not to know that two days later he would be on a breathing machine fighting for his life. His family still holds this against me and cannot understand why I did this.

Following this the hardest decision was in the hospital, I was on my own, my children had been staying at my in-laws while I stayed at my husband's side. That Tuesday morning they told me they were going to put him on a dialysis machine as his kidneys were not functioning properly and it was important that we kept the environment germ free. So I went home at 4 am to get cleaned up, it was some instinct that told me to clean up my house as well. I went to my in-laws to pick up my kids and drop off them at school. From there I made my way to the hospital.

I sat there beside him holding his hands and getting reassuring words and glances from the nurses that were with him 24 hours. I admired them, they never left their patients for one second and gave the entire necessary medical assistance like clockwork. Again it was amazing at how well they coped with everything. Also while I was there 3 people died in the ward. One was a young mother who had come in for a simple operation. I still hear the cries of her children today. "But she was supposed to be coming home Daddy, what's wrong with her?" I just wanted to reach out and hold the two girls. Their father was struggling to keep his emotions in place and console them. All my memories of when I had lost my mother came flooding back. Why does this happen, I kept thinking, it was like a vicious cycle and I could just see their future for a second.

The doctor came to see me around 9 am and told me they would be ready to put him on the machine but were a bit wary of the fact that his blood pressure was not stable and that once he was pricked with a needle the bleeding would not stop. I sat there all day, the nurses got me drinks, and I just could not leave him. At approximately 3.30pm the doctor took me to a room and asked if I wanted anybody there. Well I knew that my kids would still be at school and his brother was at the business but I assured the doctor I was okay. He then told the news I had been dreading, that I could choose to have the machine switched off now or wait till the rest of the family was here. He said that my husband taking the last breath would vary from the time that the machine would be switched; it could take minutes or hours.

My heart died at that moment, how could I make a decision like that? He assured me that my husband was not breathing, it was just the machine. It must have happened at some point today but I kept hoping and looking around to see if they were bringing the dialysis machine. I started to argue and say that there must be something that they could do, but he told me that four of the major organs were not functioning and the other were strained, had it only been two organs they may have done something. In a trance I called my brother-in-law, I could not speak and managed to tell him to get everybody there as soon as possible.

The doctor had said that once the machine was switched off it could take 20 minutes or more than two hours for the last breath; he also said to keep talking to him as he could still hear me. I asked them to wait till the family was here. When I looked up and saw that everybody was there, the nurse caught my eye and nodded. I can't recall if I responded but my head just shot back to my husband's face. There was a mixture of blood and liquid continually flowing from his mouth. I just kept wiping and whispering that I loved him and for him to be at peace. There were so many surrounding the bed now but they just seemed in the distance, all I was looking for was my children, but they could not get to me because of the family and other people that were there. Everything was a blur in the next five or six hours, up until he took his last breath. I felt as if I had just taken a huge breath myself.

It was only months later when I had time to think of what had happened surrounding his passing and realised just how much strength you would need to make a decision like that, to have a machine switched off so that an individual stops breathing. It just astounded me and unless you have had the experience nobody, well I think nobody, could explain in words just what an impact that decision has on your life and emotions.

I kept thinking that I should have asked for some more time, to put him on the machine anyway, anything but not to have given up. I don't know, but then again somehow you do have an inner voice telling you the right decision, which you ignore until it gets to a point where the words automatically come out and before you realise it, you have made the ultimate decision on another human life.

SEVEN

Demons At The Door

Thoughts of how we had lived for the last few years since my mother had passed away kept reappearing in my mind. The saddest, challenging and most traumatic moments were with my father trying to address his drinking problems.

Since my mum had died, he would be okay for a month and then drink for a month. I knew he had nobody he could talk to, no close friends or family with whom he could share his feelings. I am sure that, deep inside, he was grieving a lot.

Many times I wanted to hold him and tell him that I would always be there for him, that we all loved him very much and would not want him to go through this alone. I wished he would pick himself up and get on with life, for his own sake, if not for ours. I would look at him and think ' what is in your mind right now? What are you thinking of for the present and the future? Please see that we need you, please be a father and a mother figure to us, you have the opportunity to do this, so do it!' But I couldn't say that to him.

My father was from a generation and family background that did not express emotion and, most certainly, did not cry in front of anybody. I still remember his face on the day of my mother's funeral, it was stern and he was concentrating on doing the things that the priest asked him to do for my mother.

After the funeral and the twelfth day I walked behind him in the garden with a bucket of water to have the traditional cleansing bath in his clothes. This was supposed to wash away all connections he had with my mother, which I thought at the time was stupid. I was fascinated with everything that was going on, but also felt sorry for my father for having to carry out all these rituals.

He was unique and awesome in his own ways. I admired him for his style in clothes, different to most people, but always smart, clean and ironed to the last crease. I admired his choice of food, the way he walked like a king, proudly smoking his pipe with hands clasped behind his back, his gold 24 carat buttons, his cravats and felt hat. His style, positivity and attitude demonstrated that God had definitely created a unique soul.

When sober he was awesome! He would want a cup of tea at six in the morning and for this he needed a bottle of full cream milk. My mother made sure he always had this and, later, so did we. If the milkman was ever late, one of us would run to the newsagent like a maniac to get it for him, otherwise he would go berserk, swearing at us all. That's when we kept out of his way. The tea was really strong and you could smell it all around the house. He would boil the mixture until it was half reduced and then drink it using a saucer. The pots were burned black, but that was his breakfast tea and, along with a few biscuits, it would keep him going till lunchtime.

It was frightening when he was drinking, he would not eat properly or even have his beloved tea in the morning. To talk to him was impossible, he would not listen. He drank until he had used up all his allowance and then would resort to buying drink on credit from local shops.

I could understand that he was having difficulty coming to terms with Mum's death, but he didn't make it easy for his children to get on with life as normally as we could.

I remember having to lock him in his room so he would not sneak out to drink. This is something I would not wish on anybody, I can still hear him shouting for me to let him out. I hated having to do this, no child should be made to do this to their parent, but if he was left to his own devices he would injure himself or simply disappear and get very, very drunk.

This was something that haunted me for a very long time. At first I locked the room with a padlock, but he used to pull the door so hard that the lock broke. Next I tied his door handle to my door so that he could not get out and fall down the stairs during the night. It was horrible to do this to your own father, to a loved one. I used to feel tormented and my brothers were angry with him for making this necessary.

The hurt we felt during these periods is inexplicable, but the hurt was because every one of us was struggling with the situation and did not know which way to turn to help Dad.

If I let him out he would get to the front door or the back alleyway. Sometimes I would hear the alley door shut and just catch him before he hit the road. He did this once when there were riots going on and we were searching for him for ages, scared of what may have happened to him. Sometimes I felt it was hopeless and blamed Mum for leaving us to deal with this and then angry with God for our situation, my life just seemed like a vicious circle.

When we managed to stop him from having a drink for a while it would be a very sad and emotional time for us all. He suffered with withdrawal symptoms and would be delirious or have a terrible fever during the night. My brothers would take turns to spend time with him at night, Manish slept in the same room as my father and he was amazing to Dad and a tower of strength, urging him to get better.

When I coaxed Dad to eat something it was wonderful to see him asking for food and especially his milk for his morning tea. Each time I saw him dressing up to go for walks again and could cook for him again I felt really proud of him. Despite all his faults, we all loved him, when he picked himself up again and again we saw that he was, at least, trying.

I would pray that this time it he had to stay like this, but that never happened, there was always a next time. I used to wonder why he couldn't see how much he was hurting us. To see somebody you loved reduced to a helpless drunken state was so painful.

One of the most hurtful moments was when I saw him one day after school and looked at his watchstrap, he was wearing an ordinary leather strap. My father had a 22-carat watch and watchstrap so this really shocked me. He had had the watchstrap forever, as part of the dowry when he married my mother and I could not understand why he was wearing an ordinary strap.

When I asked him where it was, he said he could not remember what he had done with it. I was really upset and angry and called my elder brothers, they tried to get it out of him, but he was not going to tell us. I asked him the next day and he said he would try and get it back, but he never did. I ran to my room and cried at what life was throwing in my path. I had tried to do everything right by my father, making sure I provided for him as my mother had, always trying to ensure that he did not want for anything, but it felt as though nothing was ever enough

For the first time it hit me hard, like a slap in the face, I imagined back to all the challenges and traumas my mother must have gone through in her short-lived life. At that point all I wanted was to have my mother back again to look after her now, give her a better life and make sure that she did not suffer any more. Why couldn't God send her back? I still hoped and prayed that this was just a dream.

Dad had lost a lot of weight and was drinking more and more in the later years, however he had managed to cut back a lot during my wedding period. My brothers had told me that he had let go of everything after my wedding and had felt a sense of relief that he had fulfilled the promise he had made to my mother just before she died, that he would never leave us until I had gotten married and settled. She had been worried about an Indian girl and me being as young as I was without a mother's guidance in my time of need.

Despite all this the guilt I felt after my father died only added to my loneliness. Being married and in a house full of people did not stop me feeling lonely. I was grateful that he had passed away peacefully and not suffered as my mother had for endless months.

My husband had not even spoken to my father properly, other than the quick hello before and during the wedding, so he never really got to know him. Later on in my married life I was glad that my parents were not there on this earth to listen to comments made by my in-laws family about our poverty, how we lived in a shanty-like home and that I had never brought enough dowry with me. That they would never know that I was not allowed to drive the car, because it was not mine. I was glad that my parents were not alive to hear all that.

I covered up the hurt by hardening my feelings. This was easy, because I had done a lot of it in my life and it was what had got me through life. Even though I hurt painfully inside, I was strong enough to show that it did not bother me and carried on as normal. Sometimes in life this is how you get by. I told myself that I had a roof over my head and a family; some people around the world had nothing other than what they stood up in, so I was very grateful for all that I had and I still am to this day.

When I discovered that my husband also enjoyed a drink, from overhearing a conversation he was having with his father, I almost panicked. I prayed that he would remain in control of his intake. He was a joyful and humorous person naturally and would be even more so when he had a drink. The only problem was if he did have one too many then he could become irritable and loud. In the early years of our marriage and during the beginning of our business, it wasn't a problem.

He always worked really hard to help me make a go of what we wanted, and to make the business more successful. The only issue was that he was used having lay-ins in the morning and a siesta in the afternoon. I worked long hours, but it was okay as then I would have a little time to myself later, to ensure all my housework and kids were sorted before going back to relieve him. This meant that we could write the stock list, stack the shelves, empty the van (if I had not already done so during the quiet period in the afternoon) and, of course, deal with our customers.

I promised myself that I would not pressure him into giving up his drinking or cutting back. I did make him aware of how I had struggled to help my father control his drinking, because I knew no other way. His intake increased gradually over the years, but it was not the drink that contributed to his temperament. He was naturally short tempered and would go through phases where he would be angry with me and at this point did not care who was around, be it family, customers or friends. If he wanted to shout at me, he would.

People asked why I never retaliated, but I knew him. We loved each other deeply and the great times replaced many of these negative ones by a mile. The best was when he used to tell me he loved me and I him. At that time nothing else mattered.

Six months into our marriage I discovered that I was pregnant and my daughter was born on 7th October 1985. The birth was really difficult; I was panicking a lot and after 22 hours the doctors had to carry out a emergency caesarean operation. I had to stay in hospital for 14 days and my mother-in-law suggested that it was better for me to stay in hospital as long as possible as the nurses were there to look after me.

Jim was overjoyed and had been with me through every stage of the labour. He later went on to celebrate with his closest friends until the early hours of the morning.

The baby was beautiful and Jim absolutely adored her. When she was born he could not wait for his sisters to name her (as was the tradition) so that he could go and register her – and call the business after her. As mentioned earlier we named her Kajal.

Jim saw her as his lucky charm, and she has always been that to us. She has my looks, but definitely has the strong character of her father.

The pressure of the business didn't help, we were now running it from 8 am until 10 pm Monday through to Sunday with a midday break on Sunday between 2.30 pm and 5.00pm. We continued with this from 1986 through to 1999. For quite a few years before that Jim had worked within the original business, so it must have been tedious for him at times as he was a very social person and loved to mix with other people, especially his friends.

Once Jim told me that he had wanted to join the army, but was not allowed and at times he resented running the business. I wanted to do as much as I could so that the pressure was off him.

The other reason I wanted the business to succeed was for his family. They seriously doubted his ability and I wanted to prove them wrong. I felt very proud when he used to tell them how well we were doing. As all the takings went into one pot, it was like a family achievement. It was an Asian tradition that families did stick together. His family was mine now, so I wanted them to feel proud of me.

I was very conscious of doing the 'right' thing. I went to extreme lengths to keep everybody happy; I didn't care if this meant that I did without something. He resented this, and I didn't blame him, because, as the years went by, I realised that I was probably paying a little less attention to him and was more worried about others. It was important to me that others had a good opinion of us, especially his parents.

As I did not have my parents any longer, I transferred my affections to my in-laws and I loved them very dearly. I wanted them to treat me like they treated their daughters and not like a daughter-in-law. What they thought mattered to me more than anything else and we consulted them about everything, whether this was buying things for the flat or going shopping. My husband would go with his parents to purchase whatever was needed.

I loved going shopping with my mother-in-law, just to spend that time with her. And I loved talking to my father-in-law about cooking and about his boyhood when he had struggled to travel from India to Africa and set up a very successful business with his brother with no resources. If his recollections were even half true, I learned that his children didn't have the same get-up-and-go that he must have had at their age and even younger. Both my parents-in-law were very hard workers and I had nothing but the utmost admiration for them.

I carried on as happily as I could pretty much living from day to day. Then, when I was twenty-three, we discovered I was pregnant again. We were ecstatic – this is what everyone hopes for – a family and a brother or sister for my daughter.

My son was born normally after quite a painful labour. Of course, I had not rested much during the pregnancy and the doctor said that this increased the severity of the labour. I suppose I was stubborn and just wanted to keep everything going on as normal, instead of asking for time to rest.

Even on the days before I was due to go into the hospital for the delivery, I made sure that there was plenty of stock, so my husband would not struggle. As always I would plan weeks ahead; as soon as I knew something had to be done I would not rest until it was completed.

I didn't realise at the time that I was using visualisation techniques – seeing it in my head until I achieved it. Today I know that it is important to dream and visualise your goals, it helps to see where you are going and belief becomes part of your daily life.

We called my son Bhim and he was only 3 months old when it was confirmed that he was asthmatic. Jim was also asthmatic, but continued to drink and smoke regardless, I had hoped that our children would not inherit this. Jim suffered terribly with hay fever throughout the summer and often with bad bouts of flu. He also had a bad back and would be unable to work because of this for several days at a time.

I sometimes wonder how I got through these times. I carried on despite having no breaks; tiredness was not an issue with me. My mission was to keep the business running, to take care of my children and my husband and ensure that his family was happy, no matter what!

My son being ill was a real challenge, asthma is hereditary and having him in the business where the doors were constantly being opened did not help. I used to keep him in a Moses basket behind the counter, dressed up warmly. When we were really busy I would get friendly regular customers to keep an eye on him, while I served others. One of our customers used to take my daughter to the park and play on the apparatus equipment with her.

The businesses next door also had children the same age and they would come to play with our kids. I recorded lots of cartoons and children's films to keep them occupied while I was busy in the shop.

When Bhim's breathing made him struggle to sleep at night, I would have him sleep on my chest so his chest would remain clear. Despite everything I tried to ensure that my children had a normal life like others. I didn't want them to be restricted just because their parents were stuck in a business all day.

They were both were enrolled in a nursery from the age of two years old. It was only for three hours a day, but it did them the world of good and gave them a break from being in the business all day.

* * * * *

About 14 years later we decided that we wanted to live a normal life and opted to lease the business against everybody's wishes. The kids were older, we wanted to be able to do things together and I knew that I would get a job. Despite everything going on in my life I had gained my qualifications as an accounting technician so I knew that we could make a go of it. Jim seemed to be feeling the strain as the years went by, he was sleeping longer hours and did not seem as motivated.

We sold up and bought a house, although we had the rent coming in from the business we still had a couple of mortgages to pay and it was important that we started to work immediately. I got a job as Finance Officer in a community project and got my husband a job as a community worker, which he loved as it meant mixing with people all day and that was what he really good at. The first year went smoothly. Despite living in separate homes we still lived as one family with my in-laws and the kids were happy because now, instead of having to do things most of the time by themselves or with just my husband or me, we were now able to do this things as a family of four, eventually making it five with Pat, my neighbour.

Pat was 69 years old and her husband Brian was 68. We had met them when we first moved to the house, they were our neighbours. We took to them immediately and although we exchanged greetings, gifts and the fact that they looked after my children after school when Jim was away, we felt that we had known them all our lives. However, it was not until after Brian's death that I really became close to Pat. When Brian passed away Jim was really upset, as they had become close friends too.

Brian passed away in my arms while I was carrying out CPR on him after he had suffered heart failure. From that day we promised Pat that we would be there for her always, only realising at the funeral that they had no other family only friends and neighbours. We ensured that at least for the first six months that one, if not both, of us spent at least a couple of hours with her each day no matter what the circumstances. She started to accompany us wherever we went and soon it came to a point where we did not do anything without taking her into consideration first.

While I used to be at work my husband spent the time teaching her how to look after the garden, DIY and would take her places to get all her plants.

During the second year I found Jim drinking more than usual and I feared that he may not only be endangering his own life, but also the lives of the people that he drove around during the day in his community work.

I confronted him, but he denied drinking during the day and said he would stop. He often believed that I was doing things behind his back, such as seeing my family. I assured him that I would never do anything that was against his wishes and I didn't, but he was getting more and more paranoid. I knew deep down that he did not really mean anything bad, it was just his upbringing had taught him to be this way. I still loved him, and there was no doubt that my love for him was for eternity as his was for me.

EIGHT

The Door Slams Shut

In November 2000 Jim decided he wanted to go to India for a holiday before thinking of starting up in business again.

We decided that he would go first with Bhim and I would follow suit with Kajal as I had had a job offer to start in the New Year and my daughter had exams. Following this my mother-in-law and her eldest daughter decided to join him so I opted not to go.

There was something nagging away in my head telling me not to let him go, but there was no reason for me to stop him. I kept telling myself that everything was okay; he'd been on holiday on his own before. When we were running the business we couldn't both go away at the same time. I kept the business running in his absence, with help from his father or his brother when I asked them.

Finally, the day of his departure came. We had an argument over something trivial. I was telling him to be careful out there and not to drink too much and that triggered it off. But when he came to leave we hugged and I told him to look after our son. He seemed preoccupied; I think it was with all the travel arrangements and the fact that now he also had to look after his mum and his sister.

During the period that they were gone I realised just how much I loved him. I missed him intensely and would wait every day for him to call me; it was like going back to the time that we were courting. I wrote everything down on paper, as I had done then, and sent this to him. It was amazing that my feelings were so strong after all this time and I could not wait for him to get back home.

Bhim returned earlier with my mother in law and his aunt, because he had to go to school. I was worried when he told me that his dad was drinking continuously there. We had friends who were also in India at the same time, Navin and a few others were there; they told me the same thing. They admitted that he was taking medication with his drink and was hallucinating at night. I told them to bring him back. I just wanted him to get back home safely.

He had been away for a few weeks and when Navin brought him home, I was I shocked at how he looked. He had lost a lot of weight and had insect bites on his legs that had become infected. I was speechless, but kept my thoughts to myself. I was so relieved to have him back home that I tried to ignore the rest.

After a couple of weeks, he had got back into his normal healthy self. I suggested that it was time for him to go back to work, but he said he was not yet ready. One day I came from work and realised that my worst fears were confirmed. He was drinking quite heavily, starting quite early in the day.

Although this was all horribly familiar, this was my husband, not my father. I didn't know how to handle the situation until he started to complain of stomach pains, and then I knew he needed professional help. I came home one day from shopping with the children and found him in the corner crying from the pain. I took him to the emergency doctor and they confirmed that he had damaged his liver. With the amount of drink that, by all accounts he had consumed whilst in India, it wasn't surprising. The drink there is not safe and often contains pure alcohol – which can be lethal. The doctor said that, unless he took action to stop drinking, he was looking at no more than ten years more to live, maybe many fewer.

I held him that night and told him that I was scared of losing him as well as my parents. I told Jim that I needed to spend the rest of my life with him, not just a few years. For the children's sake, and mine, I begged him to seek some advice and get better.

From the time I lost my mother and at times when the pain I was feeling inside became unbearable, I would visualise my death and the funeral. I could see people looking down at me and admiring me for the things I had done in my life. At this time, as I had done many times in the past, I prayed for death. I did not wish to see another person that I loved more than my own life going through that trauma again. It may have appeared selfish, but I knew my kids would survive, as there was a lot of family that would look after them. But I was at the end of my tether and I prayed to God every day to take me from this earth.

The months went by and that summer it looked as if things were improving, but I was wrong. Jim had become weaker, but was such a strong character that he never showed anybody what he was suffering.

Any help I suggested was thrown back in my face. I couldn't do it for him, it was entirely up to him to make the commitment. All I could do was tell him how scared I was of losing him. I could not imagine my life without him. I could not believe that this was happening to me again; I had lost my parents how could I be losing the next most important person in my life?

Although he had cut back a lot on the intake, the damage had already been done during his time in India. The years 2001 and 2002 went by in a blur. In November Jim was admitted into hospital, because he had been continually vomiting. The paramedics came and told me that they would have to take him in to check why he was vomiting blood. The children came with me and stayed with him all night. In the morning I told him that I would tell his family that he was in the hospital, but he got upset and said that he did not want anybody to know. This year alone he had been in the hospital twice already and did not want to inconvenience anybody. 'I'll be home tomorrow,' he insisted.

So we respected his decision and did not tell anybody. I regretted this later, but it was what he wanted. Two days later they put him on a breathing machine in the intensive care unit. I was shocked, we had only spoken just a few hours ago, now I had to tell his family. How was I going to justify him being in the hospital for two days without them knowing. He had deteriorated during the night so they took immediate action, but I knew nothing about it. When they called me in the morning to come down I thought it was to pick him up.

I found the courage from somewhere, and I don't know how, but I drove to his parents' house and told them. Immediately I sensed the tension there and knew that they resented me not telling them sooner. I prayed silently as we drove to the hospital that, as soon as Jim was off the machine, he would tell them it was his decision and not mine.

That day never arrived. On 19th November 2002 my husband, my darling, passed away after spending six days on a respirator. He was just 46 years old.

Those six days and nights I spent beside him. I did not want to leave him for one moment. My strength came from the nurses that were with both of us for 24 hours a day. While I was beside Jim three people around me died and one started to recover. I dared not think of what may or may not happen, but prayed for him not to suffer any more. Over these days the tension had increased, it was like all my in-laws were on one side and I was on the other, even my children unaware of the tension as I had no time with them sided with them, because they knew no better. They had been there when I had promised not to tell anyone Jim was in hospital but did not realise the impact of the decision.

The twelve days of mourning after Jim died were the worst days of my life; even worse than when my parents had passed on. .My father had been through the loss of his life partner, now it was my turn.

I was really scared; I had to sit in a corner being hugged by hundreds of people that I hardly knew. It was as if I was watching everything that was happening from above. I could not believe it. I hardly saw my kids during this time and had never felt more alone in my entire life. I felt as if I was suffocating.

It was about three weeks later when I finally realised that I was alone. There was only me and my two children at home, no husband, no father, no soul mate. I cried every night on my own; never in front of the children, never.

I was weak, desperately seeking answers each day. I spoke to God angrily each day and to my hubby. How could he - in fact, how dare he - leave me like this. We had promised a lifetime together. I felt betrayed and hurt so much, like a continuous stabbing inside of me. The future frightened me, I feared for my children and the impact this would have on them.

Each day I would suddenly realise just how I felt very much alone I was again and sought out people to talk to. I just wanted someone to reassure me that everything would be okay.

As I had watched my son on the day of the funeral carrying out the rituals I saw myself back in time at my mother's funeral. I cried silently and looked down at my husband lying there in the coffin. Why did you do it, why did you break your promise and leave us? I desperately wanted everyone to leave the room so that I could be with him alone, but that was not going to happen. I had to share my last moments with him with hundreds of people. I realised that I was now back to square one, alone with two children to bring up.

How was I going to get through! I looked at my husband again and promised him that I would not allow them to grieve for their father all their lives, as I had with my mother. I would teach them to appreciate and remember all the good times we had and to keep him living forever in us. I would help them to keep a picture of him, laughing, embedded into their memory to look at and make them smile.

I would give them the love of two parents and, although I did not know how yet, I would bring them up to be two amazing human beings. I knew that this was going to be a lot more difficult now than during my father's time. In the Indian culture a widow is expected to live a lower profile life and had to be accountable, not only to society, but to all the immediate family.

That year was the hardest of my life, as soon as the funeral was over there was a conflict over the ashes. I knew that Jim wanted his ashes to be scattered in India, but his family's views were different. They wanted them to be scattered in England, in the river Thames. The tradition is that wherever your ancestors or immediate family have had their funeral held or ashes scattered then that is where the rest of the family should be laid to rest. As all their ancestors had been cremated in India I could not understand why they wanted to scatter his ashes in England.

The children and I said that we wanted to take him to the North of India where the waters of the Ganges were the clearest and the settings beautiful and peaceful. His family wanted him here, because all the family lived in England and if they died here, they did not want to be trekking all the way to India to be scattering ashes.

I lived in fear for months because of the confrontation we were having. It was me against all of my in-laws and many other hypocrites in the community that were just feeding themselves on all that was happening in my life. I could not understand why they could not respect my children's wishes and support us in this last thing that they wanted to do for their father.

I was not sleeping. I was calling people just to have somebody to talk to, but people outside, including my family, did not want to get involved. I had had numerous talks with my husband's family and always walked away without a decision being made. In the end I plucked up the courage, talked to my children and booked flights to India; something that I had never done in my entire life before.

I was so scared of telling my in-laws. One day I found the courage to tell them; it did not go down well. I could feel the hatred. There were accusations flying about. In the end I told them that they could have the ashes, but we were still going to India to do the rituals and I just walked out. I realised that I was constantly living in fear and still trying to do the best for others. I would have to pick up the ashes from the funeral directors for them to do this – so they still hadn't finally decided until that happened.

I felt for his parents and could not understand that, after living with them for nearly twenty years how they could just reject me. If I had been their own flesh and blood would it have been the same? His parents were my parents, which was all that I had known since the age of eighteen and I did not want to hurt them any more, as I knew that they were grieving for their child.

Five months later, when still no decision about the ashes had been made, I was ready to go to India. I wanted to carry out the ceremony on Jim's birthday.

Strangely Jim's first cousin had also passed away. He was the one that had been in India with Jim on that fateful trip. It was odd that they were there together and now had died within five months of each other. They were really close and I had the highest respect for him.

There was a something going on, every time I entered the room things would go quiet – I could feel it as the twelve-day mourning started. Then, after the funeral, his eldest child came to me and said he wanted me to do him the greatest favour ever.

'Will you allow Uncle Jim's ashes to be scattered with my father's ashes, on the Thames?' So this was the way his family were going to win the fight for the ashes, it was very conniving.

By this time I really did not have any more fight left in me. I realised what was happening, but was too tired to fight on my own any more, so I agreed. Kajal was so confused she did not know what was happening. Bhim, who was on a school trip, was extremely annoyed at the decision, but gave in, as I told him to.

They scattered the ashes on the river Thames the day before we flew out to India.

Taking the children to India on my own was a real scary thought. Not only had I never arranged a trip before, but had never travelled on my own, let alone this far. I was afraid of something going wrong, because this was the first thing I had done against everybody's advice, including that of my own family.

It took a long time to reassure the children that, although we did not have their dad's ashes with us, he was with us in spirit. I explained that he knew that what we were doing for him would give him peace for eternity.

My heart was ripping inside to see my children's faces, especially these last few months since their father died. They had not even had time to acknowledge what had happened before all the palaver started. The friction between his family and myself; the arguments, the fight for his ashes, the lack of support from the people that we thought were there for us when their dad was around. They were confused and looked more frightened than me. Because of them I had to put on a brave face and, even though at times I did not know what I was doing or what was going to happen, I had to give them the impression I was in control and everything was okay.

During this trip I learned a lot about my ability to do things. It was a big step, but I became more responsible and somehow gained the independence and confidence that I had lost over many years by submitting to everyone else.

I felt as if I had been guided to do this. Sometimes I shocked myself, especially when I answered back to people telling them that, regardless of their advice or wishes, I was going to make the trip.

I knew I had to go to India to do this for my husband. It was important that the kids felt they did everything that was possible to give their Dad the best farewell, and for him to be at peace for always.

Sometimes I think that when we are in dire straits and don't know which way to turn, we really do need to stop and listen to our inner selves. I did, and the courage, knowledge and answers just kept coming. Sometimes I did not know where I was getting the strength do all this, but definitely knew that whatever I did - no matter how big, small, or scary – it was the right thing to do.

During the trip my insides were in turmoil and all I did was pray that my kids would remain healthy throughout the visit, the last thing we needed was for any of us to fall ill. The whole journey was mystical, I constantly felt as if there was a hand guiding me each day. It was a funny feeling, but I felt such calmness when we got there.

The ceremony took place on Jim's birthday as planned; even though it took us just over three days' travel to ensure we got there on time. The night before there had been a problem with the vehicle that we had hired, which took several hours to repair, so we were late for the ashram that we were going to stay at. We ended up sleeping in a barn-like ashram using something similar to potatoes sacks as blankets and sleeping on cowpat.

We could not stop laughing. I told the kids that they would remember this night forever and would appreciate all the nights in the future, as it would be much better than these circumstances. I was really proud of them both; they never once complained and just adapted to wherever we ended up. Once we were there beside the Ganges, it was beautiful. The clear calm, yet strong waters were soothing. To see the sun rise against a huge statue of the Lord Shiva, someone whom my husband totally believed in, was mind-blowing.

I knew Jim was with us, that what we were doing for him was the best thing ever. It was so profound, the day was just filled with so much abundance and when everything was completed I knew that the rest of our journey was going to be wonderful.

Then we had to go back home to England. I watched the children slip into a withdrawn attitude and they told me that they really did not want to go back to that environment. I felt this so much more than them and wished that the trip would never end. I knew that it was inevitable and facing reality was going to be really tough.

I was right, it was tough. Each day I wished that I was somewhere else – away from the town where I had been happy and now was so sad. I felt myself sinking and knew that I had to do something or I risked becoming ill and hurting the children more. My life seemed meaningless.

When I was back on my own having to bring up to children, I felt as if history was repeating itself. It took a long time to come to terms with what was happening around me and I was so confused at first. Things were different to what I was used to. I had moved from the loving environment my mother created, to having to grow up immediately and take on responsibilities, but sharing so much love with my family, then living in a much more formal environment with my in-laws who were the complete opposite to my family. Now I had moved to yet another stage in my life – but I still hadn't quite accepted that.

I was always worrying. I went to work then came home and locked the door. I lived in front of the fireplace in my pajamas, watching anything that came on television, unless I really had to go out. I think the only thing that kept me from going crazy was knowing that I was also responsible for two more lives, our children. I cooked and ate with the kids, exactly the same way as I did when Jim had been around. He had loved good tasting food and my children did too.

I continued to do those same things we had done every day, so that they did not feel his loss too much. I knew from my personal experiences that I must not allow my children to grieve alone and feel totally lost. I wanted to show them that, no matter what, I would always be there for them and that life carried on. I wanted them to know that the people we lose through death are still around us in spirit and we should always treasure and remember them through the happiest and greatest moments that we had the privilege to share with them.

I used to call family and friends just to talk to somebody, but I soon found that they were all busy in their own lives and did not need me calling them all the time. It was really silly because, if I did not call them, they would say I did not want to know them anymore and, when I did call them, I could feel that they did not really want to talk. I couldn't win.

It was the same when people came to visit me, there always seemed to be an atmosphere in the room. But I was glad of the visits, as I knew it was important for the children to be in a normal environment as much as possible and keeping communication going with the outside world was vital.

Today I am glad of the experiences I had when I was young. Even though, for many years, I lost a lot of connections with the outside world and with my family, I realised two years after my husband's passing that, if I survived through all my trials as a child with minimum resources, then I could do much more today. It was like I was back to square one only this time it was with my children rather than my brothers. They say if you have done something once in your life you can do it again only better, and to never under-estimate your abilities.

I felt as though people's attitude had changed towards me; conversations did not flow freely. Why does this happen when somebody dies, why do other people's attitudes change? I knew I had to distance myself from this and finally decided that I did need somebody to talk to and have a friendship with, but who? I could not trust most of the people that offered their sympathies as I quickly discovered that anything I discussed was repeated to others. I would find this out painfully whenever there was a conversation with people that I was wary of; they would let slip something that I had discussed with others in confidence and whom I trusted.

This was more evident after Jim had passed away. It seemed that, instead of trying to understand what I was going through, people would intentionally do things that would cause me more worry and increase my vulnerability. They actually played me off against each other. I did not realise that this was happening to me at the time; I did not judge people and assumed anyone that I came into contact with or already knew were genuine in what they said. I didn't realise that they were not the people I thought they were. All I desperately craved at that time was to be loved and understood by somebody, for somebody to acknowledge what I was going through and offer a shoulder of support.

* * * * *

Eleven months after my husband passing, his sister passed away. I was shocked. I did not know what to do; just a few days earlier, on my daughters 18th birthday, I had had the biggest row with my husband's family. I felt awful at the time and did not know what to do now. I rang around friends and my family asking for advice and some moral support but did not receive any.

I knew I had to go to my in-laws' house and to London, where she lived, to pay my respects, but more so for the children as it was their aunt.

Shaking really badly, I got dressed and we went to my in-laws' house. My brother-in-law's kids started shouting at me, asking me what I was doing there. Jim's sister started firing accusations at me in front of my children. It was horrific, but I had to stay there for the children, for my in-laws and for his sister, she was a great person and we had had some great times before all this negativity started.

I just sat there quietly. I did not know what to do; they all hated me. Although that did not matter, what was important to me was that my children had to witness all this. I felt so ashamed, I should never have done anything myself, I was wishing at this point that I had done everything the way they wanted, so that I would not be in this position today. No matter how awful it was, I could not leave.

The worst was yet to come. They agreed to allow me to go to London, but to be ready for a cold reception. I was just glad that they were allowing me to go and I did not think anything more of this.

So I went the following day and the atmosphere was horrible; I felt so alone and everybody ignored me. I wanted to run from there, but what about the children, it was their father's family, their family, and they did not want to be there on their own.

Later on in the day, the family called me upstairs. Simply and horrifically, they accused me of causing her death by upsetting her parents a few days ago and did not want me there. They asked me to leave. I was on my own and I don't know how many of them were in the room, my children were downstairs. I begged them not to do this, pleaded with them, for the sake of Jim and my children, this was going to hurt them terribly. I did not even consider my own feelings, it was my children and how they would take this that worried me.

They asked me to leave again and I did. I was so upset that on the way home late at night, I got lost in the forest for over four hours. I was so afraid; all I wanted to do was to wake up and for this to be a bad dream.

I was angry with myself for not doing things the way they wanted. I was hurting for my children who were innocently sleeping in the car, unaware of what had happened, and I was angry at all the people I knew that did not even give me the little bit of support I needed. I know if there had been somebody else in my place they would have walked out of the situation long ago, or crumbled under the pressure.

I did not sleep at all for the next few days, I just kept going over in my head about what had happened and visualised the worst. I wished that the ground would open up and swallow me. How much more was destiny going to try me? How many more challenges would I need to face? When or how was my life going to change paths? Where did I go from here?

What kept going on in my mind was that they had actually let me drive home after putting me through all that emotional stress. Were they not worried about my children, or how I was going to get home? With grace, I got home safely that night, but I kept thinking to myself that, if anything had happened to my children, how would I be answerable to my husband.

They called me few days later and I was told that I would be allowed to come to the funeral because people would be asking where I was and they did not want to face up to all the questions as to why I was not there. However, they also asked me to keep away from the body. I felt like vermin. I didn't know what was right or wrong, all I knew was that

I had to do right by the children. I did not want them in the future to think that they did not pay their last respects to their aunt.

Doing all this was probably the hardest thing in my life as yet and I did it by burying all the hurt and embarrassment I felt. Despite the negative environment, I still did what I thought was right and according to tradition. Now I think of it, I shiver and wonder how I had the determination and courage to see it all through. I had to meet hundreds of people there at the funeral and pretend that everything was okay and I was there because it was my duty and the norm.

When I told Kajal and Bhim what had happened they were very angry, especially when I told them that I had literally begged for forgiveness, not knowing what I had done wrong. I was angry with myself much later on for giving in as usual and vowed to never reduce myself to that low level again. To feel so degraded is something I will never repeat; I will never put myself down at anybody's feet and submit to being told that I am not allowed to do something, no matter what. If there was ever a situation like this in the future then, hand on heart, I promised myself that I would turn around and walk away.

I know now that you do not have to be at somebody's house with hundreds of people around you to pay respects, you can do that silently in any place and the soul will know.

NINE

Going Inside

I thought I was coping really well, but found that I had been lying to myself. I was alone again and this time it felt that I had the whole world against me. I felt so lost and thought that this time there was no other path, although I had family and friends, in reality there was nobody that could understand me, the experiences I had gone through and the emotional journey I was going through now. It brought back all my memories of when I was young when I had thought that the situation then was the worst ever. This was much worse.

After I got married it was better not to have friends, except for Kiran. I tried several times over the years to build close friendships with a various people, but I just cannot seem to make that bond. I don't know what it was that prevents me from forming those relationships; I am okay when I see the people in generally social settings, but if they ever suggest that we meet up for a coffee or get together in a more specific and friendly social situation I have alarm bells ringing in my ear.

Is it that I am still frightened of commitment, or losing that time with my family, or my husband or my children? Is it that I am afraid of coming out of my comfort zone? When it comes to making a commitment like that I am afraid to do it. If I dig down perhaps I still fear that they may not like me and feel guilt because I should really be looking after those for whom I am responsible. Having put it down now in this book I know I should come terms with these feelings, but also know that the path is going to be a very hard and long one for me to change my views unless a miracle happens.

During the time in the business I did crave friendship at times, but also would know I would never have made a move. There was one lady, Amit, that used to come to the business; she used to look very down or depressed at times. I got talking to her one day as I did with a lot of our customers and she was very upset. She talked quite rapidly and, I don't know what it was but, I felt sorry for her and, oddly, given my previous feelings, a strong connection.

Through the business we built up a friendship, I felt very safe in her company. She was middle-aged, quite chubby and had four children. On reflection, she was a lot like my mother used to be. She did not go out or want anything out of the ordinary and she was very happy to be at home, which was also my comfort zone, so we had a lot in common.

We just used to spend a lot of time talking and she would help me out in the business if Jim was out or ill.

We did become really close, as her family did with my family through the business. This was really reassuring and I felt good because my husband approved of her and I felt really safe with this relationship. Because of this Jim occasionally agreed for us to go out for a meal, which was absolutely fantastic. But even while we were out I would be constantly calling home to tell them where we were, how long we were going to be, when we were on our way and finally I would be better once I was back at home in my comfort zone.

I used to feel so guilty for arranging to go out, that I would ensure my husband and the kids had similar food to what we would be eating and always brought something back for them. The minute I used to walk out the door, I could not wait to get back in and I still do the same today. My kids get annoyed and tell me off, what was the point in taking hours to get ready and then not staying for more than an hour at any event, be it family or otherwise?

Looking back, just giving her a hug used to remind me of my mother's hug. It's funny that I had never thought of all this before, but now I see that I probably attracted that mother figure because I needed somebody in that role.

My next best companion was my neighbour, Pat, whom we first met when we leased the business and bought our first home. Pat was a tower of strength for Jim while he was going through his illnesses. Again she was a mother figure in our lives, I could talk to her at any time about anything, and although she could not do anything she just provided me with all the strength I needed to carry on especially after my husbands' passing.

Whatever she learnt from my husband and whatever time we spent with her after Brian had died, she repaid me back a billion times over when Jim passed away. She never once let me give up hope and urged me to carry on living the way I had with him, as that was what he would have wanted and also for the sake of the children.

However, immediately after my husband's passing I desperately was seeking some other guidance, but I did not have any idea what it was that I was looking for. There was absolutely nobody I could turn to. I did not want to burden Pat.

I was sinking fast, especially as I was dealing with the dilemma of my husband's ashes, other ceremonies that had to be carried out and my children's future. For some reason, the thought kept coming into my mind that my life was not over yet. I still had to live and I was still responsible for our children.

Although the thought of ending my life continued to pop up regularly, I discovered that I did not really want to kill myself; I just wanted some release from the grief and pain I was experiencing. So at times I may have felt that I wanted my life to end, but I did not want to leave my children and I would feel very angry at my husband for leaving us and, more so, for allowing my children to grow up without a father.

Then, one day, I contacted a clairvoyant to seek guidance as to what was actually going to happen in my life. I know it is not what many people believe in and I was against such things myself, prior to that time. I don't know why I suddenly felt the need to get this kind of guidance, but, all of a sudden, I felt a deep spirituality. I needed guidance and this opportunity presented itself – I had to follow it up.

I was so used to following others that I was finding it difficult to make decisions myself. I had to make them and make them quickly to retain my sanity and bring some stability into my life.

At the end of my visit to the clairvoyant she gave me a recorded cassette tape of the reading. I listened to that tape five or six times a day. She had predicted an abundant future for me; according to her my life was going to be profound.

I had gone for a reading before, but I was desperately seeking a path for my life. In between breaks and before my children got home, I would listen to the words clinging to anything positive I heard. I did this for more than two years, continually visualising the events she had predicted. Those words got me through some really traumatic times.

Everybody has their own ways to get through bereavement and I had thought that, as I had been through it with my parents, I was strong enough to go through it again. I was so wrong. Firstly, I could not accept why this had happened and, secondly, why I had to lose another one of the most precious human beings in my life. Today I look at the readings as some form of life saving for the strength and me that I was directed to from some sort of force that got me through those dark, lonely and confused days.

When I was really down on our return from India, I felt really weak and close to breakdown. But I still had to carry on; I knew myself and knew that I was growing weaker by the day. The tension with the people around us was getting very heavy and I found myself losing control sometimes.

My children and I slept together on a quilt on the floor for many days. Sometimes it was just reassuring to be together, the bleakness of the future would not seem so bad then, also the companionship we gave each other meant we did not have to be alone that often.

I was determined that they did not spent that much time on their own especially in the early years when I knew they were most venerable. Kajal, especially, needed that togetherness as she was constantly having nightmares. Bhim would have them on the odd occasion and I found sleep often evaded me as I constantly had thoughts of worry, anxiety and negativity. Sometimes at night I was afraid to close my eyes.

One day, whilst getting ready for bed, I found the leaflets that the doctors had given me at the hospital; I looked at them and saw that there was a bereavement centre. The next day I called and they connected me with a lady called Debbie. They must have heard the urgency in my voice because Debbie quickly made contact and we arranged to meet.

I have never looked forward to coming home as much as I did for Debbie's meetings. They usually allocate a councilor for six weeks, but Debbie spent nearly a whole year working with me. She felt that there were so many issues and that I needed as much time as possible. She also wondered at some points whether I would ever have a breakthrough, but fortunately I did.

What I learnt from my experiences, both with Debbie and with the clairvoyant, is that even though you do not have anyone, if you crave for that support, companionship and love, the universe will deliver it in some shape or form. For me it was the one person at a time in each stage of my life for example, my mother up until the age of 10, my friend Kiran from 14 upwards, my friend Amit from being around 30, Debbie, when I knew I was going to break down and Pat who has been there since we were leased the business and moved into our first home seven years ago, during and after my husband's passing.

* * * * *

When I was married I remember going to visit my family and getting the impression from some of them that I really was not their class anymore. This used to make me feel left out, especially at family occasions. My in-laws could not have been more different from my own family, but the reflection of my 'increased' status, didn't compensate for being excluded from both my own family's loving affection and also still not being treated as a full member of my in-laws' family. I was lost in limbo somewhere between the two. I could see the preferential treatment others would get and would feel hurt and rejected, but I did not let them see this and would continue to do my bit as if nothing had happened.

Although I dearly loved all my friends, my family and my in-laws there was always a sense of discomfort around them. Maybe I felt vulnerable, as I was a widow when those around me still held their status.

There was still friction between my family and my in-laws; most of my family had only met my in-laws at my wedding and again, eighteen years later at Jim's funeral. As I was the first person to lose a partner it was very hard for my family to understand the extent of my grief. Jim's friends did try and get me out of the hole that I was digging myself, but never really offered the support that I needed because they just couldn't imagine how I was feeling and did not try to understand either.

I became more aware of how many couples there were around me all the time, doing things together and I would hurt very deeply knowing that I had lost that part of my life. Somehow people seemed to be more of a couple now then before, or maybe it was I, I just had not noticed it before. I told myself this over and over, but it didn't make the hurt any less.

Despite the issues I had with my in-laws I ensured that my children still visited their grandparents as often as possible. It was much harder to find the time, as there were always things to do after work. Whatever we did, it was never enough.

I was still studying, my children had their activities and then there was Pat to consider; I had to speak to her at least once a day. I tried to visit my own family sometimes, but they were also busy so it did not happen very often. However, it was a 100% improvement, because I had only been able to see them once a year, if that, before this.

As I was the first to lose a partner from either side of the family and or among my husband's circle of friends; it was very difficult for anyone to understand my emotions or find ways in which they could support me. For years I just tried to keep myself to myself, staying at home unless I really had to go out and I was content just to have Pat next door for companionship.

On a number of occasions Pat urged me to try and do things with other people, to make friends so that I would have some sort of life, she used to say, 'I know you, if you could you would spend the rest of your life in your home sitting by the fire.' That was true, that was the way I had planned my future, as soon as both kids were educated and established I would then retire, do some charity work and just live the life of a recluse.

Pat was not going to let that happen; she was adamant that I take some form of action and even suggested that I move to the outskirts of our hometown. She was aware of how paranoid I had become about people visiting me, I was frightened of opening the door and jumped to the window when a car door closed or people were talking outside my home. I knew I had to take action otherwise I would have become disabled by my inability to leave the house.

Since my husband had passed, I had mentioned to my children more than once that I wished that I could move away from this town. Surprisingly, I discovered that they agreed with me. I could tell by their faces that they had had enough as well and were crying out for a change in their routine.

Three years later, in 2005, Kajal started university in London. When I asked her how she was getting on, the first thing she said was 'It's amazing, there is no worry of bumping into anybody that you know, you can do what you like. But, most of all, you have peace of mind. Why don't you move here, Mum?' I thought to myself 'I need to take action', but could I take this huge step? I made a plan of the steps I would need to take, but first of all I needed Pat to approve.

She encouraged me to do it and pointed out that I was not leaving the country, but would only be a few hours away. So I made the decision and told my in-laws. At first I don't think they took me seriously, but I started to look for property and they realised that I meant to make the move

It was all new to me and I explored all the possibilities. I would trek down to London on Saturdays to view houses. It was tiring and I felt so guilty for leaving Bhim behind on the days that he had too much homework, he too was tired of the travel and the trekking. I was exhausted and I did not know London at all, other then when I dropped Kajal at her North London University. I had to decide on whereabouts we would live. I asked Bhim which college he wanted to go to and I chose an area somewhere between that and Kajal's University to look for a home.

Of course, the houses in London were double the price, but I did not let that deter me in any way. Deep down I kept telling myself that things would be more than all right. I had no idea from where I was getting the inner strength, but I had it and it was an amazing power!

I had already spoken to my manager at work and he had told me that I could get a transfer to the London office, but that they would not pay for my relocation. That was fine and at least I had a job to go to. The next step was to sell my home. My home sold in April and, as I had nowhere else to go, I rented a flat for a few months until my son completed his exams. It was convenient for him to have his own space to study in.

Those few months in the flat had probably been the most daunting of my life, as I slept there quietly on the floor watching my son on the mattress on the floor as well. Sometimes I wondered what I had done; I was here in this flat with no furniture (as it was all in storage), no visitors (other than Pat) and my heart just cried out for my children. I could see in their eyes some doubt and uncertainty about what we were doing, but they never complained. They totally believed in me to make the right moves and guide them safely to their future.

I cried a lot during those months. I kept telling myself that I was much stronger than this and knew that, now I had made this commitment, there was no turning back. I had come so far, not only risking my future, but also taking the children's lives onto a path to the unknown. Pat was my strength, especially after the conflict I had had with my in-laws on the day that we had moved out. My mother-in-law had said some very harsh words to me, but I don't want to remember them.

As she was speaking I said nothing, but kept looking at her, thinking 'I have and still do regard you as my mother, why are you hurting yourself with all these vile words, how can you possibly accuse me of so many things and have so much hate for me?'

The dislike in her eyes was destroying me inside. I felt for Bhim, who was standing there listening to all this. Once they left I was really shaken and did not know what to do. I had tried to beg her for forgiveness for anything that I may have done that caused her hurt, but to no avail. They simply did not understand. What could I do to make them happy and see why I had made this decision – short of stepping back in time and going back to the way we had been? That just was not possible now after everything we had been through.

This decision was for my children, I missed my daughter immensely. The house was quiet and lonely and, at this point, I thought it was really important for the three of us to be together as much as we could. I wanted to make happy memories, because I knew that in my life it was the happy memories that had kept me going.

I tried to go after my in-laws as the door shut behind them, but Pat and Bhim stopped me. I wanted to hold them and so wanted everything to be back to the way things were when my husband was around in the early days, when we had the business and everybody was happy with what we were doing. But I was beginning to see that you have to move forward in life, not backwards, however painful it was.

That was it; I wondered what I should do, I prayed for guidance and, feeling very heavy-hearted, knew that I had to continue and deliver the promise I had made to the kids of getting them out of the immediate environment.

The days flashed past. I hardly saw much of my family, friends or my in-laws and I did not ask anybody for help as I did not feel that I should burden them in any way. It was my decision and the kids were mature enough to help me. The flat was simple, yet clean and more than enough for the three of us, when Kajal was home. It belonged to the nephew of my husband's best friend, Sanj, who, coincidentally, worked in the same department as me. I will be eternally grateful to him for all that he has done for me

Finally the day came, the move went really smoothly. We had not asked anybody for help and had done everything ourselves. I felt that some of my family members did not want to know in order to avoid any conflict with my in-laws. Pat and my husband's best friend came to help clear the flat out, also Bhim's friends were there bright and early, which I thought was just amazing, two children showing the value of their friendship.

The hardest thing for me was making the decision to move to London and leaving Pat behind.

We had spent the whole day with her the Saturday before Christmas, and she called me that night and said that Christmas Day did not matter anymore as she already had her Christmas Day with us. I did not like leaving Pat behind and she was quite emotional when we departed. I tried to persuade her to come with us but she kept telling me it was too late for her to uproot and settle elsewhere. But she was adamant that I make the move for my children and myself. She said that she would always be here for me no matter what. Her Christmas card that year emphasised that nothing would come between us. We had agreed that we would call each other when we could in the week, would write once a week and I would visit her once a month.

A few weeks after the move I got a call from her and during our conversation I can remember discussing how amazingly peaceful it was in my new home, with no negativity and not having to live in constant fear of doing something 'wrong', as I had in my home town. She made a trip to London on Bhim's birthday, and mine, which was very courageous of her at the age of 75. She was my tower and my strength.

Sadly Pat passed away peacefully within seven months of us moving down to London. When I heard I thought 'Not again, why me, why have I lost again somebody so dear to me?' Because she was the only true genuine support that I had. She was my angel, my guardian since the time that we first met. It felt as if I had been with her all my life and not just a mere seven years.

I still miss her immensely, but I think I have had so much experience at losing the people that are closest to me that I now just go on automatic pilot and get on with whatever needs doing and carry on living.

I had only been to visit her two days before she died. It was a surprise visit and she was so happy. Our neighbours were outstanding and they had made sure that she did not spend any time on her own over the festive period. They more so proved their friendship when it came to making arrangements for her funeral. As I was the closest person and executor to her will it was down to me to make the arrangements. The neighbours did everything possible to ensure that everything went smoothly and she had the best, most peaceful service possible.

It was hard to watch my children stand up and speak at the service, it just made me realise that, since their father had passed away, we had been to so many funerals I had lost count. I really felt for my children, it was as if funerals were becoming second nature to them. This month alone we had had three funerals, my mother-like friends mum passed away on the 1st, then Pat and then Jim's best friend's father four days later.

Pat has left me with some amazing memories, but the surprising gift of all was the security she has left my children and me: her home. When I found out I could not believe it, my goal this year was to make some extra income and she gave it to me just like that, how amazing life can sometimes be.

I just wished that I could have thanked her personally. I felt frustrated as I had been with my parents and my husband, that I had not been able to speak, touch or give them a loving hug before they passed. I used to beg God to let me talk to them one more time, just one more time, for one moment. I would have given anything for that, anything at all, but it never happened. I continued talking to them anyway as I believed that they were still with me, they would hear what I was saying

Pat also had a dog, Tommy, who was now my responsibility. I was afraid to bring him to London as he was not familiar with the environment and could easily get lost. I could not handle that as Tommy was Pat's life and joy. One of the neighbours, Rob, said to me that he would look after Tommy for me until we found him a new home.

Everybody around us knew Pat; she was a walking ray of sunshine. At the funeral service there were so many people that came to pay their respects. Jim's best friend came and also my friend Amit came with her family despite losing her mother only a few days before.

The priest told me that he felt he already knew me as Pat constantly spoke about us. He also told me that Pat loved me very dearly and he was privileged to meet me at last. I felt so honoured. I assured him that I felt the same for Pat over and over again. In his service he constantly referred to the fact that although Pat did not have any family her neighbours made up for it a billon times over.

As a 'thank you' to all the friends and neighbours that were there for me and Pat I took them all out for a meal on the day that we put Pat's ashes with Brian's grave. I am so lucky to have a community that is so dedicated to helping each other, without them I would surely not have given Pat the send-off she so rightly deserved.

So in my life I have now come to realise that, although I did not recognise it, the friends were there all the time that I needed someone, they came to me one at a time. I had very special people reserved to help me in my time of need and support me through all those times when I was so low that I had even contemplated ending my life. I was concentrating on how large the families were and how they should have been there for me, but did not see that God had other people in mind to guide me through my journey.

TEN

Opportunity Knocks

There have been many opportunities that I have come across in my life, which I have missed out on. This is because they were not my priority, therefore, I did not think of them as paths that I should be taking. My priority was to ensure that the people around me were happy and content in their lives, also that they approved of the life that I was living.

I had the option to continue to study while I was young, but chose not to so I could earn an income and spend more time at home with my family.

I had the option to fight all the way and delay my marriage, but then I chose to obey the needs of what was required of me in my culture and family environment as soon as possible. If I had not married then at least I would have been with my father in his last few days. However, the positive was that he passed away peacefully knowing that he had fulfilled a request that my mother had asked him to.

After marriage the choice of continuing to go to work for somebody else or work for the family business was a choice that I made because I wanted my husband to be successful in what was required of him. Through this I learnt to become an excellent negotiator and a very powerful sales person.

Looking back in my life the opportunities that I could have taken and chose not to are probably not worth crying over; they are in the past. 'What if', is a waste of time, especially now that I know I am the person who has stepped through the ultimate door. I have done too many 'What if's and 'Why me?'s in my life and have now got rid of them completely from my conscious and unconscious mind.

The opportunities that I did take have influenced my life to an extent that I am able to be independent today, so without realising it I was creating a secure path for us.

While I worked as a cleaner with my mother I learned how hard it was to do that. As one of the jobs was in a nursery environment everything had to be perfect, hence today I appreciate the smallest things people do such as cleaning, as these jobs are more difficult then what most people realise. People dismiss cleaning as easy, but I can tell you that it is a demanding job if you want to produce outstanding results.

By going to the church for my mum's English classes we all ended up going to Sunday school and as a result of this several of my family committed their lives to the Christian faith. People from the church visited us regularly after my mother's passing and with them they brought a tower of encouragement and strength for us all. I witnessed a miracle through my brothers and their beliefs as they recited verses from the bible to my father when he was having withdrawal symptoms from his drinking issues. Each brother would take turns and it was amazing to watch, I know my father improved considerably because of this and that he welcomed the companionship that we were able to give him in these times especially during the darkness of the night.

I had the opportunity to commit myself to Christianity, but chose not to. I highly respect all beliefs that are in our world today. I am not religious, but do believe that there is a force called God and that I do have a creator and as long as I am true to myself and do only good unto others in the right manner be truthful to myself and others then my creator will know this. I also believe now that having inner peace with yourself is important and practise this regularly. Had I known all this years ago maybe I would not have endured all the suffering as I did then, but the important thing is that I am now aware.

While at home I had the greatest opportunity of my life without realising it. Not only had I learned to run a household by managing the funds appropriately, but was also able to make ends meet when I had to. I was able to delegate chores to my brothers, sometime receiving huge amounts of resentment. My youngest brother used to throw the biggest strop. He ran away once; at first I thought it was really funny, but then realised he had really gone. When I went to look for him I found him in the churchyard at the end of the road. I was so relieved to see him, but also very angry and clouted him across his head!

I know that my parents are proud of us all because of where we are today having got through many challenges whether they were in the physical reality form or emotionally.

* * * * *

My marriage opened up a well of endless opportunities for me. Throughout the marriage I learned how the other half lived. I was able to adapt to a family that was completely the opposite from my own family. I learnt to speak fluently in the native language; I learnt to respect and earned respect so that I was proud to say I was my parents' daughter.

From my father-in-law I learnt so much history about how he grew up with nothing and with his brother became one of the most successful businessmen in our community. In addition to this he taught me how to cook the most amazing dishes and they were all favourites of my husband.

In the business I learned really good business skills and gained so much knowledge about providing quality service to others to make sure that the business would prosper. I also acknowledged my strength and power to endure long hours of working with out a break or feeling tired and my ability to lift really heavy goods everyday.

I got to know a lot of the people in our community because of my in-laws status, hence I was recognised wherever I went as their daughter-in-law. This was good at times and not so good when I needed to have my own privacy. However, it is absolutely great to walk in to an event of some kind and just see the enormous amount of people swoop around me irrelevant of their intentions.

I have the most beautiful children that were and still are good as gold despite growing up in a business environment where their parents were busy most of the day. Also taking into account the emotional ride that they have had over the last few years, I know they have come through shining. Both Kajal and Bhim are my inspiration, my towers of strength and my recognition in this society.

I took advantage of any opportunities I could do to give my children a loving, but realistic upbringing. I got them to learn to swim and achieve lots of awards, took Kajal to dancing classes, and Bhim to Tai Kwando and Scouts. They always had a few of their friends around for their birthdays and visited friends regularly, I tried to give them a normal upbringing as much as I could under the circumstances.

So in the process I may say that I became an exceptional mother and am very proud of my children and myself. They are both intellectual in their own ways and very challenging. No parent can describe exactly how strongly he or she feel for their children, but their feelings are reflected in things that they do each day.

Something that happened in the business brought the chance for me to start studying again in my early 30's. The bookkeeper had accidentally misrepresented the figures when completing the tax returns and we were in threat of having an inspection. They would review the last three years of the business and may have gone back as far as six years. We also found out that the bookkeeper had not been doing his job correctly and had put in a lot of estimates.

Standing at the Door

To justify the returns we had to prove where the figures came from. I told my husband I would start from six years back, processing all the documents. This took a few months and I was able to get as near as possible to the figures disclosed which prevented us from having a penalty notice issued. As I had thoroughly enjoyed the work I asked my husband if I could do a bookkeeping course, emphasising the fact that I would be able to get a decent job if ever we were to sell up, he agreed.

That was it, my professional career had started. The first course I did was in Information Technology as my husband wanted to purchase a computer and thought it was a good idea if one of us knew how to use one. The course got me a distinction pass.

The second study program at a degree level got me an award for outstanding achievement. I had barely attended college and did most of the theory and assignments on my own at home between 2am and 5am and when there were quiet periods in the business I was still achieving some of the top marks from our lecture groups that I had hardly attended.

When customers came in they used to admire at my determination to succeed and always asked how I was getting on, but could not believe that I was actually doing this, running the business, doing all the household chores and looking after my kids. I used to look at people that were dressed smartly for work enviously and would wish that I, too, could be like them and have that status.

I asked every professional that I came into contact with what they did and how they got there. I wished that I was there or had at least continued to study while young. I told myself that I was stupid to even think of going for a profession, let alone imagining myself already being there, but there was no harm in dreaming!

My next professional qualification was the hardest as it was something I tried to do during the most difficult time. When my husband was ill and kept failing the odd paper. If I sat three papers I would fail two and if I sat two papers I would fail one. It was very disheartening, but then a miracle happened, out of the fourteen papers that we had to pass, it was compulsory to do the final three together. When I found out I thought that was never going to happen, I would never get through all three.

While I was studying for these my Kajal and Bhim also had major exams, so it was important that I kept them well nourished and provided for them all the time they needed for studying. The household never suffered because of my studies. I would continue to do all my normal activities during the as this was one of the criteria that Jim wanted. This time during the last three papers, I also had guests staying, so tried to take my daughter to the library every day, first thing in the morning.

The result, despite all the challenges, was that both my children got through which was amazing and I unbelievably got through all three papers as well for the first time. How absolutely awesome was that? Pat was over the moon and told me she continually had prayers said for me at church on Sundays. Thank you, Pat, for having faith in me and believing that I could do this, you were my inspiration.

So that is how I got all my job opportunities after we leased the business. I started in a small community charity company, following this I went to work for a practice. This was the big one for me, not only did they expect me to do the professional qualification, but also to do every aspect of accounting. There were many areas that I had never had the opportunity to practice. This was the first time that Jim and I were apart for most of the day.

As soon as I would get into work I would call him and vice versa. I started this job while he was in India, so it was a very rough ride because of Jim going into hospital three times in the first year and his continuous illness. The partner I was responsible to was very supportive and also understood when I could not concentrate fully at work.

I continued to work there after Jim died, but found it very hard to settle. I would find myself picking up the phone to call Jim to let him know I had arrived safely. Eventually, four months later, I left, just before flying to India

Every two years or so I moved on to something more challenging and higher paying, finally getting to where I am today.

It has been an amazing journey. The dream I had as a child and never once thought that it would come true, has taken over 25 years. But I got there and that's the most important thing. What is also vital is that I never gave up and I believed in every decision I made. Sometimes I am still astonished at the progress I have made in my career. Despite having two children and working full time I still managed to be at home on their return from school and dropped them off in the morning as well, just as we had always tried to do when their father was there. My priority was my children and under no circumstances was I going to let them suffer anymore.

It was definitely a hard trek. I must have filled hundreds of application forms and attended many interviews, which were disheartening, but I never gave up hope. I knew that, although life had closed its doors at this moment, they would be wide open for me when the right opportunity came and so they did.

It was only now that I understood what my father must have gone through when my mother had died. He was very quiet at times and feel now that he may have been dying little by little as time moved on, I don't know.

Because of my experiences with losing first one parent, then the other – and then my husband, people call me when they have lost somebody dear and tell me they know exactly how I must have felt then. Sometimes they apologise for not trying to understand me better before jumping to the conclusion of ignorance that I did not want anything to do with them. Maybe if they did I would not have contacted Debbie, who knows? However, having Debbie was a real gift and I would recommend anybody that needs help to seek it, because help is there for you if you choose to take it.

I suppose everybody has their own way of dealing with losses, but I know for sure that, no matter how well people appear to be coping, they will probably need some support some way or the other. It's unwise to over-estimate how well anyone is dealing with grief, but good to let them know sincerely that you are there, if and when they should need you.

Immediately after someone's loss it's unrealistic for things to be normal. They may try to carry on day to day as if nothing has happened, but all sorts of things will be going on in their minds, from pain to numbness, from disbelief to acceptance. A friend needs to be understanding and let them have a little space to grieve and then gradually to help them to build up enough confidence to try and get some normality back into their lives.

This type of support would have reassured me that there were people who cared for me and were there if I needed them. It would have been so much easier knowing that they would be there to help me when I was ready to take the next step.

I know that I have tried to take advantage of all the opportunities that have come my way in my career and have been fully committed to all my working environments. However, my journey has brought me to now – when I have decided to develop myself on a personal basis. This stage will generate that confidence that will enable me to connect with people in a way that will make an impact in their lives.

Nearly a year ago I met up with my brother who looked totally energised. He told me he had been to a seminar, which blew his mind and had changed everything for him. He asked me if I would like to go to one and, just seeing the change in him, I said yes without even considering the costs. I thought that it would be a break for the kids and me and it be good to do something together.

However, a few months later, when I found out how much the tickets were, I told my brother to cancel, but it was too late. At this time I still had not asked what the seminar was all about.

When I got there at first I was just glad to be in a different environment, but over the next few days I found that it really was a magical ride for those that went with an open mind and participated fully. The seminar was called Unleash the Power Within and its presenter was Tony Robbins.

I have never looked back since. It has opened huge, and I mean **huge**, doors for my children and me in every part of our lives. It is very hard for me to explain the transformation that took place. From a suicidal state of mind just one month before the event to the success I am today, I would say that I believe it was my destiny to be there.

I knew nobody in London on a professional or friendship level when we moved here, but I have made hundreds of friends because of the connections through attending various seminars and now, with my children, am a volunteer in all the events that I can possibly be in, meeting and helping others in any way we can and giving back some of the experiences back that we received.

I don't think there is a better way or environment for getting my children started in the right path of their lives. They absolutely love it and I am so proud of them, especially when they get up at 5 am and do not go to bed till well after 12 am for a number of days when volunteering and, believe me, they are still so full of energy afterwards – amazing!

ELEVEN

The Door To A New Life

Moving to London was a huge turning point for me. Arranging everything for the move was like when I had arranged to go to India, everything just fell into place and I can tell you I was so grateful to God for that. Once we were in the house I thanked him for everything, not only walking each step of the way with me in the past and the present, but also for the future. I knew then and still know that he will never let me down, and will carry me when the going gets tough. This is what I believe in and I have total faith in my creator.

It felt strange for me to rediscover this deep faith, because for years I had stopped believing. It was so weird, because the moment I started communicating with my inner spirit and reaffirming my faith again, things began to move. This is why that now, not only do I think it is important for me to have faith and belief in my creator and universe, but also in myself as I am the creation and have a path that I must follow. You can say that I was reaching out for my dreams and because I saw myself taking the steps to make them real. I achieved them.

Once we were in London I was able to think more clearly almost immediately and noticed that I was already in a much more peaceful state. My job was awesome and being in the city made it all the better, but I knew it was not what I really wanted. Within months a better opportunity came and I took it. The new job gave me status beyond any of my expectations and allowed me to put my professional skills to good use and achieve my full potential.

The environment is amazing; I get to see Big Ben everyday and hundreds of tourists! When I see their faces and the excitement, it brings back memories of what it was like just a few months ago when we were in a different position. I don't take it for granted, as I love the buildings in London and spend ages just walking around them. What really fascinates me is how each one has been built and designed, they truly are unique and I would have loved to have seen them being built. I feel privileged to see the gifts that these past generations have given us with their amazing talents.

In the month we had moved to London, I came across a newspaper advert offering a free seminar on coaching. This was something I had never considered, but thought it could be a way of meeting people in London and may help me to build up my confidence levels too. So Kajal and I attended this free course together.

The presenter was Mike Loyns at Catalyst Coaching; he was an excellent presenter and really held my interest. I went home thinking that the course would be good for me to do as a personal development process. I spoke to Mike and he helped to arrange some financial support. I could not wait to get started, I had become so used to studying and sitting exams that I was addicted! I needed to get back on track again!

I joined up and set my goal of completing this within four months. I knew it was a tight goal, especially with the job, the new environment and supporting my children, but I thought that if necessary I would work during the early hours of the morning, as I had done in the past with all my professional exams.

The last year had been tough; not only did I have the final three papers for my accountancy qualifications, but also had to do my Diploma at work, which included a huge portfolio of evidence. The exams were really close to each other i.e. three in one week and the diploma papers the next week. I still can't believe that I got through all of them at the first attempt, it was easy. Now I knew I had what it took to be successful at a high academic level.

I did all the modules, practice clients and theory work well before the time expected. My mentor Vicki Ross, an excellent coach, mentor, master Neuro Linguistic Programming practitioner/trainer was fantastic; she guided me step by step offering me advice and support whenever I needed it as did my dear associate during the seminars Gary Duff-Smith. They also let me practise full board and the constructive feedback ensured that I became the perfect accredited coach!

Looking at how successful Vicki is in her business has only encouraged me to emulate her. As I was Mike's first student to be accredited in their company, they offered me the opportunity to help facilitate future training events and to become a mentor.

Mike has been a tower of inspiration and encouragement during my studying and still continues to support me. He's given me so many opportunities to take part in different types of work within the same field. His wife Meera, whom I met at the first module, was very genuine when she told me that, Yes! I would achieve my goal of completing the course within the time period that I had set myself! It's hard to fail with that kind of belief and confidence around you. When I spoke to her during a practice coaching session I saw in her eyes just how much she really did believe in me and I felt that I had to do Mike and Meera justice by succeeding in all my goals.

The colleague that I instantly built up a bond with was Gary as mentioned above, he encouraged me to do well at every step and we completed the course together, supporting each other from start to finish. He has become a good friend and we still help each other to develop our skills and knowledge.

Following this course, I met up with a very dear friend I had met in Fiji in one of Tony's seminars. His name is Pa Joof. He was my guardian angel at that time in my life when I was totally confused, yet trying to get my life together but not really knowing the direction. Pa has stopped me from making impulsive decisions and has guided me to becoming a property investor today. He has been instrumental in many of the things that I am and will be doing. He is my inspiration; when I see him I see an aura of light surrounding him. My children deeply love and respect him. I believe that we were guided by a force to meet and will be eternally grateful to him for all the support and guidance he has and still does provide for me.

Under Pa's guidance I signed up to attend a business-training course with the business magnate and expert Keith J Cunningham. I'd heard Keith speak and talked to him briefly at one of Tony's seminars; now I know him personally!

The course was amazing and very challenging. Keith is an excellent down-to-earth teacher and makes it simple enough so everyone can understand the concepts of a successful business. He made it even more special by making us accountable to our own teams for the next 120 days.

This was the time period he had set for us to establish, achieve or learn about where we wanted to be in the future. All who attended promised commitment and I knew that I had to pull all the stops out. Because of this commitment and the fact that I would be answerable to all when the time period finished, I would definitely be doing something that would make me proud of whatever it was that I finally achieved.

It was amazing; here I was in London seven months after moving here and I had taken vital action and produced these fantastic results. I had obtained a top job in central government, which gave me the opportunity to develop myself as an accountant. I had become a property investor with a developing portfolio that would be security for my children and would make me financially abundant. I had qualified as an accredited coach so that I could help others who are also seeking guidance in some shape or form. The coaching has given me the opportunity to become a facilitator for training coaching events and become a mentor for trainee coaches. All these things were light years from my life before the move, they are simply beyond anything that I could possibly have dreamed of. I even use my skills in all the contribution work I continually do, be it for children or HIV sufferers.

TWELVE

Many Doors

Reflecting on what I had been through over the years, I knew that the kids had been struggling to come to terms with losing their father and the friction that was happening now with the families. I encouraged them to spend time with their friends doing things that would take their minds off their loss. We did try to do more of the things that we used to do with Pat, such as going out for meals, visiting the cinema and charity events. I racked my brains to think what I could possibly do to bring some laughter and fun back to their lives.

I thought back to my time when we were grieving and very lonely. I tried to think of the little things that brought me moments of happiness. Other than having a big family where we did have a lot of fun, our pets bought us a lot of joy and happiness. Pets can bring happiness and comfort into our lives with out even saying one word and allows you to love them unconditionally.

Looking back to when we were young, we had always had a pet, sometimes more than one at a time. We had a dog, fish, hamsters and cats. I spent a lot of valuable time with my pets, especially when I came home early from school Dad used to be sleeping and I was alone. The cat was always in front of the fire, so, after doing all my chores, I would pick him and put him on my lap and there we would sit for hours and watch television together. My brothers and parents all loved pets and they had always been a part of our lives ever since I can remember.

One day, when we had the business, I had suggested to Jim that we should get a dog, as he was always going on about owning one. He was really excited about the idea, but then told me that he would only walk the dog and I would have to do the rest, such has training him, cleaning up after him and all the other things that need doing for dogs. I didn't mind at all because I adored animals

We bought a Doberman; it was from a customer who bred them. He was absolutely beautiful and a delight to have but, unfortunately, although he was a puppy, he was very big and would snatch the baby soother from Kajal's mouth! We were worried that he might bite too hard one day and we were getting busier in the business, so trying to watch the dog and my daughter at the same was extremely difficult. In the end we thought it was safer to return him, it was very sad having to let him go but knew he was going to a really good home.

We had two more dogs after this; both German Shepherds. The first one was white and we only had him for a very short time, as the original owner's son was missing him so badly that I returned him. The next one was called Sheroo, which means lion. He was my baby from the age of eight weeks. I used to watch my husband taking him for walks; he felt so proud walking him, but really he was mine! I took him to training classes, where, of course, he did everything he was not supposed to do!

I walked him morning and night no matter what; the first walk at 5 am and the last at 10 pm, just before or after the business closed. I used to wash the kennel and the yard every day so he was in a clean environment and I bought fresh food for him, even though he ate a lot of the food I cooked for the family as well. Pat's dog, Tommy, had never eaten dog food in his life and expected everything to be freshly made, talk about being spoilt.

Sheroo needed a lot of care and we gave him everything we possibly could because to us he was part of the family and, to me, had a heart

Standing at the Door

and soul just as we did. When I got up in the morning or returned from the cash and carry, he would be waiting, wagging his tail rapidly with excitement and you could see the love and welcome shine brightly from his eyes; he was adorable. It's very hard to explain the connections that you have with animals, but I knew that what I had with my pets was extremely special.

He would sit beside me all day in the business, he would walk beside me whenever we went out and when he was extremely ill, I brought my bedding down and slept beside him until he recovered fully, he was my true companion especially when I was feeling down. Jim had a massive special kennel built for him, his only failing, if you can call it that, was that if anybody ever left the garage doors open to get stock he would sneak in and do his business, which my father-in-law discovered many times, much to his disgust.

So thinking of how much pleasure pets had brought me I wondered if this would help the children to recover in some way from the loss of their father and have the privilege of giving love unconditionally to a pet. I asked them if they would like a pet. They both wanted a dog, but I told them that it was much harder to look after a dog, especially as we were all out during the day and it wasn't fair to leave a dog alone all day. Besides every one on our road, including Pat, had dogs and cats, which we could play with at any time.

I suggested a rabbit at first, they thought I was kidding, but I promised that if they could look after a rabbit properly then we might consider a dog later, when we could find a way for it to not be alone all day. I would have loved a dog too, because I just absolutely adore them, but I knew that our current circumstances would not allow it. I took them to the pet shop in less then a hour we were back home with a baby rabbit that was boisterous and had stripes like a tiger.

Obviously, we called him our darling Tigger and two years later he is naughtier than ever and thinks he owns the house. He has his own bedroom, loves honey and oatmeal cookies and chapattis where he always burns his mouth by eating them too hot. He can smell me making them a mile off and clambers around and around my legs until I give him one with a very hungry or, should I say, greedy expression in his eyes. Tigger is just like a dog – as soon as he hears one of us come in he will run to us and start nudging our feet, so cute and clever!

It's funny though with animals of all kinds, I can tell when they are content, angry, tired, sad, happy loving and so on. I look at Tigger sometimes and wonder at the ways he has turned our lives around completely. He is house trained and waits by the door to be let out, also being the softy that he is, he allows the squirrels, crows, and pigeons to eat his food. He has made us look forward to coming home, just to see his look of relief, as if saying 'thank you for coming back'.

He has made the kids more responsible and allows them to express their care and love openly, in fact, I forward my gratitude to him for all that he has done for us in providing the love and joy that he so easily gives us and allows us to return it to him many times over.

Pat adored him and looked after him while I was at work and even if, sometimes, we were away for a weekend, she loved the challenge as he was quite fast and would run around her, she absolutely thought he was the funniest little thing around and never thought that she would care for a rabbit in this life. However, I don't think Tommy approved of it much!

Once we had Tigger everything revolved around him, especially when we moved to the flat and the new home, it had to accommodate him. I felt it was important for him to feel as comfortable as we were and he loves the new home. We are lucky to have a farm behind our house where he goes to board when we are going away or crewing for a Tony Robbins event. It's really funny because he is so used to being in a clean environment that, as soon as we drop him off, he starts to clean himself and is quite rough when we pick him up, usually in very grumpy mood for having left him there in the first place.

Getting the children a pet did wonders for them psychologically and physically. They now have something to take their minds off other issues, which has made them become more independent and responsible.

I love watching them clean his hutch out or the garden area for him; the care and consideration they show him and his environment is amazing. Also when I am late from work or attending some event, Tigger is a great companion. We are still planning to get a dog, I already see us playing and messing around with him on a sunny beach with waves crashing on the sand.

So my future does have my dog in it and possibly other beautiful animals that we can give a loving home to. Sometimes I put my head right next to my pet's to see if I can try and home in on their thoughts, they never move away, but cuddle up as close as they can. Perhaps they know that I am just sending them love vibes!

Saying all this I realise that pets are not for everybody and it's important to seek advice and look for a pet that you can look after.

* * * * *

My future will evolve because of my continued positive attitude towards life and how I can change it. It is very important for me to keep my inner wisdom on track by continually developing myself, which, in turn, will allow me to accomplish exactly what I want. I ask myself daily:

What is my truth?

What is the imprint I want to make on this world, as a parent, as a friend, as work colleague, as a boss, as a child, as a lover, as a partner?

What is the statement or concept that I believe in so strongly that I will dedicate my existence to it? Is it compassion, empowerment, protection or love? Is it gentleness, wisdom, lightheartedness, or strength? Is it grace, will, integrity or optimism?

Since this is my truth, I have the ability to change it, tweak it, harness it and make it soar. But it is virtually impossible to keep it to myself, because, with each breath I take, I interact with the universe and the truth, which flows like a ribbon through my daily existence.

Since doing my first UPW (Unleash The Power Within) I have, each day without fail, asked myself the ten empowering morning questions written in one of Tony Robbins' books. In addition to this I continually recite a few words from Napoleon Hill's book. Having reconnected with my spirituality, I connect with God every moment and believe that as his representative on this earth, his powers flow through me in all that I do.

These things I do daily, because it enables me to keep on track of my new found life; a life where it does not matter what the issues are I will live my life to its full potential. I have had an amazing journey, so far, and know now that each step of my past has made me the stronger person that stands tall today. I am grateful for each experience and the challenges that the universe has put to me. I faced those challenges with courage and, deep down. I knew that, even when I felt like giving up, I had never really lost hope, no matter what the situations were.

It is that inner strength that you don't realise you have until you dig really deep into your soul. My future now will be what I make it and there is absolutely no negativity in my path. At present my next biggest challenge is taking part in the marathon, again this was a dream I had as a child which I have realised now and am doing it for a very special charity. I can't wait to be with the thousands of courageous people taking part and know that the day will be out of this world; I also know that I will complete it, although I don't know in how many hours!

I have so many ideas of where I want to be and what I want to do that, sometimes, I feel as if my head will explode. It's this newfound belief that I can do whatever I want and know that I have the ability to do it. Obviously, I will not attempt everything under the sun, but will definitely follow the goals and paths that are dear to my heart. It is as if I am back to my teenage years and have the opportunity and ability to do all the things I desire and, believe me, this time round I will open the door to my profound destiny that is filled with so much abundance.

I sponsored a little boy called Nadungu in Nairobi with the donations I received at my husband's funeral and still continue to provide the support today. I support a vast number of charities, as that is something I am very passionate about and have done so for most of my life. But now I can also commit the time physically which is so much more rewarding to me.

I chose a child in Kenya because it is my birthplace and I have committed to visiting him in the near future, which, in turn, will allow me to visit where I was born. That will be really exciting, especially to see the ground where my parents lived for the first part of their lives as a family. It will truly be an experience for me to be there and visualise what was happening so many years ago and where my life on this earth began.

THIRTEEN

The Door Into The Future

I have been through a very complicated, yet exciting, journey of life to date and know that I have come through tremendously well. I want to share these thoughts and processes with you to show you how to take the opportunities life offers you. I was challenged and became a fighter. I can reassure you that if I can get where I am today, then you can also achieve your dreams.

Decisions:

Every time I have to make decisions throughout my life I always had to put myself through a drilling process. I'm sure most people have something similar that they do when faced with a dilemma. I ask myself 'do I believe in the decision I am about to make; how am I going to actually take the step of making it and what are my thoughts about it?'.

I probed deep inside myself to be sure I was whole-heartedly behind this decision. I considered my thoughts and whether they were positive or negative. I analysed if it was going to give me the outcome I so desired or whether I would be losing out on something else. This process is important for, if you make impulsive decisions, you may later regret it.

I often visualise the scenario before taking action and consider the reason why you do what you are doing. It is vital that you don't hurt anyone who will be directly affected by your actions; that can be a very difficult emotion to live with and can be very demoralising. Remember to consider others before taking action. However, at the end of the day you must make the decision that is right for you, not the one that everyone else wants you to take. If, it turns out to be the wrong one, at least you have gained experience and additional knowledge that you did not have before, therefore celebrate what you have learned!

I have sometimes searched for an easier path, looking at what others had done and following their lead. This has never motivated me in the long term, but has been a cure for a short-term issue.

When I think back it was a matter of making the decisions there and then with no time to think of failure. Once made, I stuck by them even though later on I may have realised that it may have been the wrong one. Pride got in the way and I attempted to see whatever I had decided on through to completion. Like I said – it was all very valuable experience.

Making decisions can have a life-changing impact, especially on people that are dear to you. Through my mistakes I have learned always to take time out and consider thoroughly what I am about to embark on, which is something I would highly recommend. The importance of considering the outcome cannot be stressed enough.

Leadership:

We are all leaders in our own way, be in a social, family or other scenarios.

When I have responsibilities and am in control of situations I know I am a natural leader. To be able to lead I know it is vital to have very good listening skills. This ensures that you hear the smallest of things that may have the greatest of effect on yourself and others. Your listening ability is the most important quality you have, as I have learned through my coaching sessions. I would have given anything to have had somebody just listen to me when it looked as if I was not going to get through the barriers that were put before me.

When I decided to do the coaching Diploma I did not realise just how intense it was. Initially, on hearing Mike speak at the seminar, I thought that I really could do with a coach in my life, but, at that point, I also knew that I could not afford a personal coach. Then I realised that training to be a coach myself would inspire me to coach myself as well as others. As I went through the modules I craved more knowledge, because I was finding out how this position had opened many doors for millions of people.

The most successful people in the world today have coaches to guide them through life. This is something you may consider for yourself, finding a coach will help you to reach your dreams.

Coaching allows you to develop personally, raises your self-empowerment and achievement. You can grow as fast as you want to and it is amazing how quickly you do, because you have somebody that you're accountable to. If you are prepared then you will have the ability to be, do and have anything you desire.

This was one of the reasons I became a coach, supporter and a mentor, just to be available to anybody that may need me to help them to push their barriers down, as I have done. I also want to coach those who do not have the means to hire a coach; that is a dream that is coming true for me in my contribution work.

Being a leader does not necessarily mean you are leading a team or a nation or a seminar. I know that it also means that you have the ability to stand alone, no matter what you are or where you are in life, be it at home, school, work, in time of distress and especially in traumatic times. A true leader will push down that door and get to the other side no matter what. I have done this so many a times in my life, despite the circumstances and pressures upon me. If you are unsure in life about anything, please seek guidance. The help is out there; just ask, for you have nothing to lose, but mountains to gain.

Action:

Deciding the actions I needed to take after making my decisions was the next big stepping-stone for me. It was easy to decide that I wanted to do something but how I went about doing it was a completely different issue. You should ask yourself constantly 'will it work?' but be careful that does not make you hesitant. You need to ensure there is not the slightest bit of self-doubt preventing you from seeing it through.

If the actions are time consuming that may put a damper on things, we are all busy and often impatient. However, you need to consider how badly you want this outcome and that will drive you to take the action no matter what limitations you have. I have discovered over these last few years that, if you do not ask, you do not get and just how true this is!

For many years I gave and gave, but never asked for anything in return, well, not aloud, but inside me I wished that I could have their love, friendship and respect. Obviously, they were not going to give something they were not aware that I wanted. So, if you want something, you need to ask. If you do not ask, you won't move forward. I was lacking in courage to take that action and felt guilt for taking anything from anybody, even if it was just advice. Get over the guilt, it is just a word!

What I have discovered over the years is that you can put a meaning to any feeling you want. You can choose how you feel about anything. If you fail an exam, you can choose to feel demoralised, sad and refuse to do a retake or feel happy that you have gained a vast amount of knowledge and know that the retake will not require so much time to study for again.

Find out what is available out there, speak to people who already have experience of where you want to be or are already successful in what you want to be doing. That's what I did; I constantly thought about how I could move forward, especially being an Asian lady and breaking away from tradition. It dawned on me that the few people I had come to know in London were already successful and very powerful, so were ideal peer groups for me You become like the people with whom you spend most of your time – so it is very important to choose who you 'hang out' with.

You have to be realistic and know that it is not going to happen overnight and that you probably still have a long way to go, but don't give up before you get started. The key is to be patient as well as persistent. I decided the coaching course was how I was going to invest in myself and enrolled immediately. It took time, it was hard and I had to be patient in the process. The only element that was 'overnight' was my study hours!

You must also remember to reward yourself every time you achieve something or overcome an obstacle, this is very important, as you are acknowledging all that you have done.

If you really want to experience more success, passion and fulfillment in your life, you need to make the commitment to identify the steps you are going to take that will make it happen. The more you live from happiness, instead of for happiness, the sooner you realise that it is your own attitude and perspective you have to change first, as I have. The chances are that, when you are assessing yourself and get feedback from others, you realise the gaps in your life. This is great, because it means that you can now do something about it.

Generate a list of options that you have, listing everything you have thought about doing now and in the future. Talk with someone you trust and who will provide honest and constructive feedback, such as your coach or mentor. This will confirm the direction that you're thinking of taking and the actions to achieve your desired outcomes are on target. Share this list with people that know you well and ask for their reactions – but not with anyone who is likely to be negative.

Don't keep looking back and wishing that you had pushed yourself a little harder. Use your peers as examples and follow their path by seeing how they have done. Make the most of what you have, get rid of all your negativity and develop your love for all humanity because that is what will give you peace and success.

Be confident and proactive in what you do, this will enable you to reach your dreams!

My footnote

Just before Christmas I set out on a particular goal, which, I thought, would never be possible in a million years. I had so wanted to write a book, but was struggling until a friend recommended the Book Midwife, a lady called Mindy.

I contacted Mindy and explained what I wanted to get down on paper, but told her how much I was struggling about getting on with it. She said some magical words; "everybody has the right to publish their book." My spirits lifted immediately and I began to see that there was hope of actually completing this goal of mine.

We arranged to meet in the first week of January, as Mindy was fully booked. My original goal was to start before the year-end, but she was really busy, 'so', I thought, 'what's a week? I'll just wait.'

A couple of days later Mindy called me and told me she was going to make it happen this side of the New Year. I could not believe it! I was so grateful and so excited. With her professionalism and expertise to guide me, whoopee, I could tick that goal off my list! I started to imagine what the book would look like and who the people that would be reading it would be. I cannot express my gratitude enough – Mindy is an exceptional person. Had it not been for her, you would not be reading this book today; she made this dream come true.

So I'm here in London, my children have settled happily in their schools and at home and our rabbit, Tigger, is content with having the whole garden to himself! For the first time in my life I have started to do the things that I really want to be doing. I have made some amazing friends during my journey these last few months, from not knowing anybody when we moved here to literally having hundreds of friends, supporters and encouragers behind me today. What a magical journey it has been for me; I believed, I visualised and I made it happen and all within one year of deciding that enough was enough and that I too wanted to live a life that was passionate and powerful where I am a beautiful soul making an impact to all those that cross my path. I have in the last year, in addition to being an Accountant, have become a successful outstanding Coach, Mentor, Master Neuro Linguistic Program practitioner, trainer and teacher.

Until we meet again!

Printed in the United Kingdom
by Lightning Source UK Ltd.
124202UK00002B/208-378/A